contents

4 THE CHRONICLE OF COCA-COLA®

8 SOUPS & STARTERS
Appetizers and small party plates

30 ENTRÉES: BEEF & PORK
Crowd-pleasing main meals

60 ENTRÉES: POULTRY & SEAFOOD
A variety of satisfying recipes

84 SIDES, SAUCES & SALADS
The perfect complement to any dish

110 DESSERTS
Tempting treats for all occasions

142 INDEX

The Chronicle of

Birth of a Refreshing Idea

The product that has given the world its best-known taste was born in Atlanta, Georgia, on May 8, 1886. Dr. John Stith Pemberton, a local pharmacist, produced the syrup for Coca-Cola and carried a container of the new product down the street to Jacobs' Pharmacy, where it was sampled, pronounced "excellent," and placed on sale for five cents a glass as a soda fountain drink.

Carbonated water was teamed with the new syrup to produce a drink that was at once "delicious and refreshing" (a theme that echoes to this day). Thinking that "the two C's would look well in advertising," Dr. Pemberton's  partner and bookkeeper, Frank M. Robinson, suggested the name and penned the now-famous trademark "Coca-Cola" in his unique script.

During the first year, sales averaged a modest nine drinks per day. Dr. Pemberton gradually sold portions of his business to various partners and never lived to see the success of the beverage he created. Just prior to his death in 1888, he sold his remaining interest in Coca-Cola to Asa G. Candler, an Atlantan with great business acumen who proceeded to buy additional rights and acquire complete control.

The Candler Era

On May 1, 1889, Asa Candler published a full-page advertisement in *The Atlanta Journal* proclaiming his wholesale and retail drug business as "sole proprietors of Coca-Cola...Delicious. Refreshing. Exhilarating. Invigorating." By 1892, Mr. Candler's flair for merchandising had boosted sales of Coca-Cola syrup nearly tenfold. He soon liquidated his pharmaceutical business and focused his full attention on the soft drink.

The trademark "Coca-Cola," used in the marketplace since 1886, was registered in the U.S. Patent Office on January 31, 1893. Mr. Candler promoted the product incessantly, distributing souvenir fans, calendars, clocks, urns, and countless novelties, all depicting the trademark.

Bottling began in 1894 and went large-scale in 1899. Over the next 20 years, the number of plants grew from two to more than 1,000—95% of them locally owned and operated. The bottlers in the early 1900s fought a never-ending battle against imitation producers, which was the major force behind the evolution of the distinctive hobble-skirt bottle. Coca-Cola deserved a distinctive package, and in 1916 the bottlers approved the

 unique contour bottle designed by the Root Glass Company of Terre Haute, Indiana.

The now-familiar shape was granted registration as a trademark by the U.S. Patent Office in 1977, an honor accorded only a handful of other packages.

A Man Named Woodruff

In 1919, a group of investors headed by Ernest Woodruff and W.C. Bradley purchased the Coca-Cola Company for $25 million. Four years later, 33-year-old Robert Winship Woodruff, Ernest Woodruff's son, was elected president of the Company, beginning more than six decades of active leadership in the business.

The new president put uncommon emphasis on product quality. He initiated a "Quality Drink" campaign to assist fountain outlets in aggressively selling and correctly serving Coca-Cola, and established quality standards for every phase of the bottling operation. In fact, Mr. Woodruff's belief in the vast potential for the bottle business took the Coca-Cola business to unrivaled heights of commercial success.

 Merchandising concepts accepted as commonplace today were considered revolutionary when Mr. Woodruff introduced them. Among the many concepts the Company pioneered are the innovative and convenient six-bottle carton in the early 1920s; the metal open-top cooler, which, starting in 1929, put ice-cold Coca-Cola into countless retail outlets; the distinctive fountain glass,

adopted as standard in 1929, which are still used at many soda fountains today and serve as visible proof of the timeless popularity of Coca-Cola; and automatic fountain dispensers, introduced at the 1933 World's Fair.

Today, modern fountain technology continues to dispense Company products faster and better than ever before.

Refreshment Knows No Boundaries

Mr. Woodruff's greatest contribution may have been his vision of Coca-Cola as an international product. Working with talented associates, he established the global momentum that eventually carried Coca-Cola to every corner of the world.

The international growth of Coca-Cola began in 1900, when Charles Howard Candler, eldest son of Asa Candler, took a container of syrup with him on vacation to England. A modest order for five gallons of syrup was mailed back to Atlanta. Distribution in the 1910s and '20s remained rather haphazard.

However, in 1926, Mr. Woodruff committed the Company to organized international expansion by establishing the Foreign Department; Coca-Cola and the Olympic Games began their association in the summer of 1928. Mr. Woodruff's vision of the international potential of Coca-Cola is still being implemented and refined by the Company, its bottlers, and subsidiaries, building the Coca-Cola business into an unparalleled global system for providing a simple moment of pleasure.

Moving with the Times

From the late 1940s to the 1970s, the United States, like most of the world, changed at an unprecedented pace. World War II had recast the world, and the Company faced a new, more complex global marketplace.

New packaging was introduced. The 10-, 12-, and 26-ounce king-size and family-size bottles debuted in 1955 and were immediately successful. Metal cans, first developed for armed forces overseas, were available on U.S. market shelves by 1960. After years of research into plastic soft-drink bottles, the

Company introduced PET (Polyethylene Terephthalate) packaging in 1977 in the 2-liter size.

it's the real thing!  Through the years, jingles and slogans have set the pace for Coca-Cola advertising. One of the world's most famous advertising slogans, "The Pause That Refreshes," first appeared in *The Saturday Evening Post* in 1929, followed by "It's the Refreshing Thing to Do" in 1936 and 1944's "Global High Sign." Many more memorable slogans followed, including "Things Go Better with Coke" in 1963. "It's the Real Thing," first used in 1942, was revived in 1969 to support a new, tremendously successful merchandising campaign.

Fine illustrations by top artists including Norman Rockwell were featured in color-ful ads that projected the product's image in leading magazines. Noted artist Had-don Sundblom's popular Santa Claus "portraits," *[right]* which began in the 1930s, continued as holiday ads until the early 1960s.

I'd like to buy the world a Coke... The deep emotional bond between Coca-Cola and its consumers grew even more powerful and more global. In 1971, young people from around the world gathered on a hilltop in Italy to sing "I'd Like to Buy the World a Coke," which offered a counterpoint to turbulent times. Advertising has continued the tradition of presenting Coca-Cola as one of life's simple pleasures, distinctive and acceptable anywhere, exemplified by "Have a Coke and a Smile," made memorable by the heart-warming connection between Pittsburgh Steelers tackle "Mean" Joe Greene and an awestruck young fan.

From Small Beginnings

The history of Coca-Cola is a story of special moments. Moments that originated with Dr. Pemberton in Atlanta and have been multiplied billions of times around the world; moments made familiar and universal by Mr. Candlers's unique advertising and Mr. Woodruff's vision to put Coca-Cola "within an arm's reach of desire." After 125 years, through more than a century of change, Coca-Cola remains a timeless symbol of quality refreshment.

soups &starters

Mini Sliders with Coca-Cola® Caramelized Shallots

MAKES 12 SLIDERS

1½ pounds ground beef

1 tablespoon onion powder

1 tablespoon steak sauce

1 teaspoon salt

1 teaspoon black pepper

2 tablespoons butter

1 tablespoon olive oil

8 large shallots, thinly sliced

¼ cup *Coca-Cola*®

12 buns or mini rolls, lightly toasted

Cheddar cheese (optional)

MIX ground beef with next 4 ingredients. Form into 12 small, even patties. Set aside.

HEAT butter and oil together in medium skillet over medium heat. When butter is melted, stir in shallots. Cook until just beginning to caramelize, then add *Coca-Cola*.

INCREASE heat to medium-high and cook liquid about 4 minutes, until liquid has almost evaporated. Return to low heat and continue cooking until fully caramelized. (Do not allow shallots to burn.)

WHILE shallots are cooking, cook burgers in large nonstick skillet over medium-high heat 3 minutes on each side. Top each patty with slice of cheese, if desired.

FILL each bun with a burger and heaping spoonful of shallots.

Crostini with Eggplant Tapenade

3 tablespoons olive oil

2 cups diced eggplant

⅓ cup diced shallots or onion

1 cup pitted kalamata olives, chopped

1 tablespoon capers with juice

½ cup red peppadew peppers, chopped with 2 tablespoons juice*

1 tablespoon balsamic vinegar

½ cup *Coca-Cola*®

½ teaspoon red pepper flakes

Salt and black pepper

Toasted baguette slices

HEAT oil in large nonstick skillet over medium-high heat. Add eggplant and shallots; cook about 6 minutes or until richly golden, stirring often. Add olives, capers and peppadew peppers with their juices; continue stirring about 5 minutes, or until most liquid has evaporated.

WHEN mixture has reduced, add vinegar and *Coca-Cola*. Sprinkle with red pepper flakes, salt and black pepper.

REDUCE heat to low. Cook until thickened, about 15 minutes. Stir several times during final cooking stage. Serve warm or cold on toasted baguette slices.

If unavailable, may substitute with roasted red peppers.

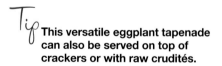 **This versatile eggplant tapenade can also be served on top of crackers or with raw crudités.**

Gazpacho with Coca-Cola® Reduction

MAKES 4 TO 6 SERVINGS

⅔ cup *Coca-Cola*®, divided

½ cup balsamic vinegar, divided

¼ cup olive oil

⅔ cup tomato or vegetable juice

⅛ teaspoon ground red pepper

3 tomatoes, seeded, cored and chopped

1 red bell pepper, seeded, cored and chopped

1 medium sweet onion

1 large shallot, chopped

1 large cucumber, seeded and chopped

Salt and black pepper

½ cup sour cream or plain yogurt

½ cup fresh basil leaves

BRING half of *Coca-Cola* and half of vinegar to a boil over medium-high heat in medium saucepan. Cook about 3 minutes or until liquid measures about 2 tablespoons.

MEANWHILE, whisk together remaining *Coca-Cola*, remaining vinegar, oil, tomato juice and ground red pepper. Pulse tomatoes, bell pepper, onion, shallot, cucumber and tomato juice mixture together in food processor or blender until mixture becomes a rough purée. (Work in batches, if necessary.)

SEASON with salt and black pepper and chill several hours. Serve gazpacho in chilled bowls with dollop of sour cream. Drizzle with cooled syrup and garnish with basil.

Black Bean Dip

1½ tablespoons oil

1 shallot, minced

2 cans (15 ounces each) black beans

1 can (4½ ounces) chopped green chilies

1 tablespoon minced chipotle pepper

½ cup *Coca-Cola*®

⅓ cup ketchup

1 teaspoon garlic powder

1 teaspoon onion powder

¼ to ½ teaspoon ground red pepper

½ cup cream cheese

½ cup spreadable Cheddar cheese

½ cup shredded sharp Cheddar cheese

Chopped green onions

Tortilla chips (optional)

Salsa (optional)

Sour cream (optional)

PREHEAT oven to 375°F. Heat oil in large saucepan over low heat. Add shallot; cook until softened.

STIR in black beans, chilies, chipotle pepper, *Coca-Cola* and ketchup. Add garlic powder, onion powder and ground red pepper. Bring to a boil over medium-high heat, reduce and simmer, uncovered, 25 minutes or until most liquid is evaporated, stirring frequently.

USING a fork or hand-held blender, lightly mash bean mixture. In bottom of 8-inch pan, mix together cream cheese and spreadable cheddar cheese; spread mixture to corners.

SPOON bean mixture evenly over cheeses and sprinkle with shredded Cheddar cheese. Bake 10 to 15 minutes or until bubbly. Sprinkle with chopped green onions and serve with tortilla chips, salsa and sour cream, if desired.

Caprese Bruschetta

¼ cup balsamic vinegar

2 tablespoons *Coca-Cola*®

Garlic powder, divided

6 Roma tomatoes, seeded and diced

12 large fresh basil leaves, chopped

¼ cup extra-virgin olive oil emulsified* with 1 tablespoon *Coca-Cola*®

1 teaspoon salt

Black pepper

¼ cup softened butter

1 French baguette, cut into 24 slices

12 small balls fresh mozzarella cheese, cut in half**

Fresh basil

BRING vinegar, *Coca-Cola* and pinch of garlic powder to a boil over medium-high heat in small saucepan. Reduce heat to medium-low and cook about 10 to 15 minutes, until mixture is reduced to a syrup. Remove mixture from heat to cool.

MEANWHILE, lightly toss tomatoes with chopped basil in medium bowl. Stir in emulsified oil/*Coca-Cola* and season with salt and pepper.

MICROWAVE butter in small microwave-safe dish 15 to 20 seconds. Spread baguette slices with butter and sprinkle lightly with garlic powder. Toast baguette slices on baking sheet under broiler about 1 minute on each side or until crisp. To serve, top bread slices with 1 heaping tablespoon of tomato/basil mixture and 2 cheese halves. Drizzle with cooled syrup and garnish with basil.

*To emulsify means to blend two or more unblendable substances such as vinegar and oil. This can easily be done with a whisk, hand blender, or food processor.

**If unavailable, may use an 8-ounce fresh mozzarella ball. Cut ball in quarters and slice each quarter into 6 slices, making 24 slices total.

Italian-Style Vegetable Soup

MAKES 6 TO 8 SERVINGS

1 package (12 ounces) uncooked small pasta shells or corkscrew pasta

1 can (28 ounces) crushed tomatoes in purée

1 can (15 ounces) white beans, rinsed and drained

1 can (14½ ounces) vegetable broth

1 can (12 ounces) *Coca-Cola*®

2 cloves garlic, minced

1 bay leaf

2 teaspoons Italian seasoning

1 teaspoon salt

½ teaspoon white pepper

1 bag (16 ounces) frozen vegetable medley, such as broccoli, green beans, carrots and red bell peppers

Juice of ½ lemon

Fresh basil leaves (optional)

COOK pasta according to package directions; drain. Set aside.

COMBINE tomatoes, beans, broth, *Coca-Cola*, garlic and bay leaf in large Dutch oven. Add Italian seasoning, salt and white pepper; mix well. Bring to a boil over high heat. Reduce heat to low and simmer 10 to 15 minutes, stirring occasionally.

ADD frozen vegetables to Dutch oven and return to a boil over high heat. Stir in pasta and reduce heat to low. Simmer 10 to 15 minutes or until heated through. Remove bay leaf; stir in lemon juice. Ladle soup into bowls. Garnish with basil leaves, if desired. Serve immediately.

Mushroom-Barley Soup

MAKES 6 SERVINGS

6 slices bacon

1 onion, diced

3 stalks celery, sliced

2 small carrots, peeled and sliced

10 ounces sliced mushrooms

1 teaspoon minced garlic

⅛ teaspoon red pepper flakes

4 cups beef broth

1 cup uncooked barley

½ cup *Coca-Cola*®

1½ cups water

Salt and black pepper

COOK bacon over medium-high heat in 4-quart saucepan until crisp and browned, about 10 minutes. Remove bacon with slotted spoon, chop into bite-sized pieces and set aside. Reserve 1 tablespoon bacon grease and discard the rest. Add onion, celery, carrots and mushrooms to saucepan. Cook about 8 minutes until vegetables are crisp-tender. Add garlic and red pepper flakes and cook an additional 1 minute, stirring constantly.

ADD remaining ingredients. Bring to a boil then cover and reduce heat to medium-low. Stir in bacon and simmer 40 minutes or until barley is tender.

Tip **Before cooking the barley, rinse it thoroughly under running water, then remove any dirt or debris you may find.**

Coca-Cola® Chili

1 pound ground beef

1 medium onion, chopped

4 stalks celery, chopped

1 can (about 15 ounces) tomato sauce

1 can (14½ ounces) beef broth

2 tablespoons chili powder

1 teaspoon garlic powder

1 teaspoon paprika

1 teaspoon ground cumin

1 can (15 ounces) kidney beans, drained

1 cup *Coca-Cola*®

1 teaspoon hot pepper sauce

Salt and black pepper

SPRAY 3-quart Dutch oven with nonstick cooking spray. Cook beef, onion and celery over medium-high heat until meat is browned and vegetables are tender. Drain excess fat.

ADD tomato sauce, beef broth, chili powder, garlic powder, paprika and cumin to meat mixture; stir well. Bring to a boil over high heat. Reduce heat and let simmer, uncovered, 20 minutes; stirring occasionally.

STIR in beans, *Coca-Cola* and hot pepper sauce. Continue to simmer 10 to 15 minutes. Season to taste with salt and black pepper. Garnish as desired. Serve immediately.

Tip **Try cooking this chili one day in advance. By cooking the day before, letting it cool, then refrigerating overnight, you give all the flavors in the chili time to blend.**

French Onion Soup

¼ cup butter or margarine

4 cups thinly sliced onions

2 cans (10½ ounces each) beef broth

¾ cup *Coca-Cola*®*

1 teaspoon salt

½ teaspoon vinegar

⅛ teaspoon black pepper

Thick French bread slices

Grated Parmesan cheese

MELT butter in heavy saucepan; add onions and cook until golden; do not brown. Add undiluted beef broth, 1 soup can of water, *Coca-Cola*, salt, vinegar and pepper.

COVER; simmer 20 to 25 minutes.

TOAST 1 side of French bread slices in a broiler. Turn, generously sprinkle with Parmesan cheese and toast until browned.

LADLE soup into deep bowls and top with toast, cheese side up.

To reduce foam for accurate measurement, use Coca-Cola at room temperature and stir rapidly.

Ginger Chicken Wings

MAKES 12 WINGS

2 teaspoons cooking oil

2 thin slices fresh ginger

12 chicken wings, just the middle section

½ cup dark soy sauce

1 can (12 ounces) *Coca-Cola*®

HEAT oil and ginger in medium saucepan over medium-high heat.

WHEN oil is hot, brown wings on both sides. (Do this in batches if necessary.) When all wings are browned, remove ginger and add soy sauce and *Coca-Cola* into saucepan.

BRING mixture to a boil, then turn to medium heat and simmer about 30 minutes or until meat falls off bone easily. Increase to high heat 2 to 3 minutes to let sauce thicken. (Make sure wings are covered with *Coca-Cola*/soy sauce mixture.) Add more sauce according to taste.

Twin Cheese Dip

MAKES ABOUT 3 CUPS

¾ pound (12 ounces) sharp Cheddar cheese

1 package (4 ounces) Roquefort cheese, crumbled

1 clove garlic

¾ cup *Coca-Cola®*, divided

2 tablespoons soft margarine

1 tablespoon grated onion

1½ teaspoons Worcestershire sauce

1 teaspoon dry mustard

¼ teaspoon salt

⅛ teaspoon hot pepper sauce

GRATE Cheddar cheese into large mixing bowl. Add crumbled Roquefort. Put garlic through press; add to cheeses with ½ cup *Coca-Cola* and remaining ingredients.

PLACE mixture in food processor; pulse until combined. Gradually add remaining *Coca-Cola,* then process until mixture is fairly smooth, light and fluffy. Pack into covered container. Chill. Best if refrigerated overnight.

Tip This dip keeps very well for a week or more. Twin Cheese Dip is good with raw vegetables, as a spread for cocktail breads or crackers, or even as a sandwich filling.

Coca-Cola® Glazed Bacon-Wrapped Dates

MAKES 4 SERVINGS

8 slices bacon

2 tablespoons balsamic vinegar

⅓ cup *Coca-Cola®*

1 teaspoon Dijon mustard

⅛ teaspoon granulated garlic

16 large dates

8 teaspoons cream cheese, divided

16 raw almonds, roasted or smoked

½ teaspoon salt

½ teaspoon black pepper

1 tablespoon unsalted butter

PREHEAT oven to 400°F. Cut bacon slices in half and cook in medium skillet over medium heat 1 minute on each side. Drain on paper towel and set aside. (Bacon should be soft.) Discard bacon grease.

ADD vinegar, *Coca-Cola*, mustard and garlic to skillet. Cook on medium heat 3 to 4 minutes or until becomes a thickened glaze.

WHILE glaze is cooking, slice one side of each date lengthwise and remove pit. Fill each date with ½ teaspoon cream cheese and 1 almond, then pinch date closed.

WRAP each stuffed date with ½ slice bacon and secure with wooden toothpicks. Remove glaze from heat and stir in salt, pepper and butter. In nonstick rimmed baking sheet, drizzle 1 tablespoon sauce and place 4 dates side by side in each.

EVENLY drizzle remaining sauce over the tops and bake 10 minutes. Remove from oven and let cool slightly, about 5 minutes.

Spicy BBQ Party Franks

1 tablespoon butter

1 package (1 pound) cocktail franks

⅓ cup *Coca-Cola*®

⅓ cup ketchup

2 tablespoons hot pepper sauce

1 tablespoon cider vinegar

2 tablespoons packed dark brown sugar

HEAT butter in medium skillet over medium heat. Pierce cocktail franks with fork. Add franks to skillet and brown slightly.

POUR in *Coca-Cola*, ketchup, hot pepper sauce and vinegar. Stir in brown sugar; reduce heat.

COOK until sticky glaze is achieved. Serve with toothpicks.

French Lentil Soup

3 tablespoons olive oil

1 medium onion, chopped

1 carrot, chopped

1 stalk celery, chopped

1 clove garlic, minced

½ pound dried lentils, rinsed and sorted

1 can (about 14 ounces) stewed tomatoes mixed with ½ cup *Coca-Cola*®

3 to 4 cups chicken broth

3 tablespoons olive oil

Salt and black pepper

½ cup grated Parmesan cheese

HEAT oil in large skillet over medium heat. Stir in onion, carrot, celery and garlic. Cook about 9 minutes, or until vegetables are tender but not browned.

ADD remaining ingredients, except cheese. Bring to a boil over high heat, reduce heat, cover and simmer 30 minutes or until tender.

SEASON as desired with salt and pepper. Serve in bowls or over pasta, rice or sautéed fresh spinach. Sprinkle with Parmesan cheese just before serving.

Hickory-Smoked Barbecue Chicken Wings

MAKES 24 APPETIZERS

2 pounds chicken wings, tips removed, cut in half

3 teaspoons hickory flavor liquid smoke, divided

1 cup barbecue sauce

1 cup *Coca-Cola*®

⅓ cup honey

¼ cup ketchup

2 teaspoons spicy mustard

2 teaspoons hot pepper sauce

1 teaspoon Worcestershire sauce

¼ cup sliced green onions (optional)

PLACE chicken wings in large resealable food storage bag; add 2 teaspoons liquid smoke. Toss to coat. Refrigerate at least 1 hour to let flavors blend.

PREHEAT oven to 375°F. Spray 13×9-inch baking pan with nonstick cooking spray.

COMBINE barbecue sauce, *Coca-Cola*, honey, ketchup, mustard, hot pepper sauce, Worcestershire sauce and remaining 1 teaspoon liquid smoke in medium bowl; mix well. Pour sauce into prepared pan. Add chicken wings to pan; toss to coat.

BAKE 35 to 40 minutes or until chicken is tender and no longer pink, basting occasionally with sauce and turning once.

REMOVE pan from oven and discard sauce, leaving just enough to coat wings. Set oven to broil and return wings to oven. Broil 3 to 4 minutes. Garnish with green onions, if desired, just before serving.

Seafood Gumbo

MAKES 4 TO 6 SERVINGS

½ teaspoon granulated garlic

½ teaspoon black pepper

⅛ teaspoon dried thyme or oregano

½ teaspoon onion powder

2 tablespoons olive oil

2 tablespoons white flour

2½ cups diced onion

1½ cups diced celery

¾ cup diced red bell pepper

1 clove garlic, finely minced

1 teaspoon hot pepper sauce

1 teaspoon red pepper flakes

1 cup crushed tomatoes, strained

3 cups chicken stock mixed with ½ cup *Coca-Cola*®

6 okra, sliced

6 slices hot coppa*, chopped and fried

1 small can smoked oysters, rinsed and drained

1 cup lump crabmeat

1 cup small raw shrimp

2 fresh Roma tomatoes, seeded and chopped

Salt and black pepper

2 cups cooked white or brown rice

COMBINE first 4 ingredients in small bowl and set aside.

HEAT olive oil in large stockpot over low heat. Stir in flour; increase to medium-low heat and cook until a brown roux is achieved, about 15 to 20 minutes.

INCREASE heat to medium-high; add onion, celery and red bell pepper. Cook until tender, about 5 minutes.

STIR in garlic; cook 1 minute then stir in spice mixture, hot pepper sauce and red pepper flakes. Add strained tomatoes and simmer over medium-low heat, 10 minutes, stirring occasionally.

ADD *Coca-Cola*-infused broth and bring to a full rolling boil over high heat. Add okra; reduce heat and simmer, uncovered, 40 minutes.

ADD coppa, oysters, crabmeat, shrimp and Roma tomatoes to stockpot. Cover and cook an additional 30 minutes over low heat. Season with salt and pepper to taste. Serve over rice or mix rice in as desired.

Coppa is a cured meat much like salami. It is sometimes called capicola or capicollo. If you are unable to find coppa in your grocery store, you may substitute with salami or another type of cured pork.

Italian Minestrone Soup

2½ pounds blade chuck roast or meaty soup bones

2½ quarts water

2 teaspoons salt

1 small onion, sliced

½ cup celery leaves

1 bay leaf

2 slices bacon, diced

1½ cups kidney beans

½ cup cut-up fresh green beans

½ cup diced celery

½ cup fresh or frozen green peas

½ cup thinly sliced zucchini

½ cup thinly sliced carrots

¼ cup diced onion

¼ cup cut-up parsley

1 clove garlic, minced

½ cup (2 ounces) uncooked elbow macaroni

1 can (6 ounces) tomato paste

1 cup *Coca-Cola*®

1 tablespoon olive oil

1 tablespoon Worcestershire sauce

1 teaspoon Italian seasoning

Salt and black pepper

Parmesan cheese (optional)

PLACE first 6 ingredients in large pot, cover and simmer about 2½ hours until meat is tender. Strain broth (should measure 2 quarts). Add a few ice cubes to harden the fat, and remove fat from broth.

FINELY dice meat, discarding fat and bones, to about 2 cups.

COMBINE beef broth and meat in 5- or 6-quart kettle. Place over low heat. Meanwhile, fry bacon until crisp. Add bacon with drippings and remaining ingredients, except Parmesan cheese, to the broth.

COVER and simmer about 30 minutes, until vegetables and macaroni are tender. Serve sprinkled with Parmesan cheese, if desired.

entrées: beef & pork

Spaghetti and Meatballs

MAKES 4 TO 6 SERVINGS

3 slices day-old Italian bread, torn into small pieces

⅓ cup *Coca-Cola*® mixed with 1 tablespoon balsamic vinegar

1½ pounds ground beef or a combination of ground beef, veal and pork

1 medium yellow onion, finely diced

¼ cup chopped fresh parsley mixed with ¼ cup minced fresh basil

1 egg

1½ cups grated Parmesan cheese, divided, plus additional if desired

2 cans (about 14 ounces each) diced tomatoes, undrained and divided

1½ teaspoons dried oregano, divided

3 to 4 cups cooked spaghetti

PREHEAT oven to 350°F. Soak bread in *Coca-Cola* mixture and heat in microwave on HIGH 30 seconds. Mash with a fork.

MIX ground beef, onion, herb mixture, egg and 1 cup Parmesan cheese together in large mixing bowl; add mashed bread. Mix until incorporated. Form meat mixture into 12 large or 18 smaller meatballs; refrigerate 15 to 30 minutes to firm.

COAT large skillet with nonstick cooking spray; heat over medium heat. Add meatballs; cook 8 to 10 minutes or until browned on all sides. Remove from heat.

POUR two thirds of tomatoes over the bottom of large rectangular baking dish. Season with half of oregano. Sprinkle with ¼ cup Parmesan cheese.

GENTLY set meatballs in rows ½ inch apart in prepared dish. Drizzle with remaining tomatoes; sprinkle with remaining oregano and Parmesan cheese. Bake 40 to 45 minutes. Serve over cooked spaghetti. Garnish with additional cheese, if desired.

Sweet and Sour Glazed Beef Kebobs

MAKES 6 SERVINGS

¾ cup *Coca-Cola*®, divided

½ cup pineapple juice

¼ cup soy sauce

⅓ cup cider vinegar

1 tablespoon Worcestershire sauce

1 tablespoon tomato paste

4 tablespoons packed dark brown sugar, divided

1 tablespoon garlic powder

½ teaspoon red pepper flakes

1 large onion, cut into 1-inch pieces

2 pounds boneless sirloin steak, cut into 1½-inch cubes

2½ teaspoons cornstarch

2 to 3 teaspoons chili-garlic sauce*

Salt and black pepper

Hot cooked white rice (optional)

MIX ½ cup *Coca-Cola*, pineapple juice, soy sauce, vinegar, Worcestershire sauce, tomato paste, 2 tablespoons brown sugar, garlic powder, red pepper flakes and onion in covered container; marinate steak overnight in refrigerator.

REMOVE steak cubes and onion pieces from refrigerator. Reserve marinade.

ADD marinade to small saucepan. Bring to a boil over high heat. Spoon 2 tablespoons marinade into small bowl and stir cornstarch into hot liquid until mixture is smooth. Return liquid to pan. Stir in remaining 2 tablespoons brown sugar and chili-garlic sauce. Reduce heat to medium and simmer 15 to 18 minutes until thickened and reduced to 1 cup. Season to taste with salt and black pepper.

MEANWHILE, place steak cubes on 6 skewers, alternating evenly with onion pieces. Broil 3 minutes, turn and broil 2 minutes.

GLAZE kabobs with sauce using a clean pastry brush. Serve over rice, if desired.

Chili-garlic sauce can be found in the Asian foods section of the grocery store.

Note

If using wooden skewers, soak them in water for 20 minutes to prevent them from burning during the cooking process.

Aloha Burgers
with Pineapple Chutney

MAKES 6 SERVINGS

2 pounds ground beef

2 tablespoons teriyaki sauce

2 teaspoons Worcestershire sauce

2 teaspoons onion powder

1½ teaspoons salt

2 teaspoons black pepper

2 tablespoons butter

2 tablespoons packed dark brown sugar

¼ cup *Coca-Cola*®

¼ cup balsamic vinegar

½ medium red onion, diced

1 small tomato, seeded and diced

1½ cups diced pineapple

Salt and black pepper

6 brioche buns*, toasted

MIX beef, teriyaki sauce, Worcestershire sauce, onion powder, 1½ teaspoons salt and 2 teaspoons pepper in medium mixing bowl and form into 6 patties; set aside.

MELT butter in medium saucepan over medium-low heat; stir in brown sugar. Add *Coca-Cola* and vinegar. Bring to a boil, reduce heat and simmer 20 minutes, stirring frequently.

STIR in onion; cook and stir 2 minutes on medium heat. Add tomato and pineapple, stir to coat and turn off heat.

MEANWHILE, cook burgers under broiler or on grill pan over medium-high heat, 6 minutes on each side. When cooked to desired doneness, keep warm. Return pineapple mixture to high heat 1 minute. Season with salt and pepper. Top each burger with a heaping spoonful of pineapple mixture. Serve on toasted brioche buns.

If unavailable, may substitute with hamburger buns.

Coca-Cola® Sloppy Joes

MAKES 4 TO 6 SERVINGS

1 pound ground beef

1 onion, finely chopped

¾ cup finely chopped green pepper

1½ tablespoons all-purpose flour

1 cup *Coca-Cola*®

½ cup ketchup

2 tablespoons vinegar

1 tablespoon Worcestershire sauce

2 teaspoons dry mustard

½ teaspoon black pepper

½ teaspoon salt

Hamburger buns

BROWN ground beef, onion and green pepper in heavy-bottomed saucepan over medium heat. When meat is cooked through, drain excess fat.

ADD remaining ingredients, except buns, and stir to combine. Cover and simmer 30 minutes, stirring occasionally.

SERVE meat mixture on hamburger buns.

Note

This family-favorite recipe usually includes ground beef, ketchup, or tomato sauce, and a variety of spices served between two slices of bread or on a bun. Sloppy Joe's are easy to prepare and budget-friendly.

Smokehouse Barbecued Brisket

MAKES 6 SERVINGS

3 tablespoons olive oil

1 beef brisket, trimmed of fat (about 3 to 4 pounds)

Salt and black pepper

1 tablespoon granulated garlic

1 cup beef broth

1 onion, minced

1 teaspoon red pepper flakes

1 tablespoon liquid smoke

½ cup *Coca-Cola*®

4 tablespoons packed dark brown sugar, divided

2 cups tomato purée

1 can (12 ounces) *Coca-Cola*®

2 tablespoons onion powder

2 tablespoons hot pepper sauce

1 tablespoon Worcestershire sauce

Kaiser rolls or hamburger buns

PREHEAT oven to 250°F. Heat oil in large skillet over medium-high heat. While heating, season brisket liberally with salt, black pepper and granulated garlic.

BROWN brisket in skillet about 4 to 5 minutes per side; transfer to large covered casserole or Dutch oven.

DEGLAZE skillet with beef broth, scraping bottom of pan. Add onion, red pepper flakes and liquid smoke. When onion is translucent, add ½ cup *Coca-Cola*. Pour mixture over meat; sprinkle with 2 tablespoons brown sugar.

BRAISE brisket 5 to 6 hours, basting every ½ hour. When falling apart, remove meat; set aside to cool slightly and add remaining 2 tablespoons brown sugar, tomato purée, 1 can *Coca-Cola*, onion powder, hot pepper sauce and Worcestershire sauce to Dutch oven. Increase heat to 400°F and cook, uncovered, 30 minutes. When cool enough, slice meat into ½-inch slices. Return brisket to Dutch oven and baste with sauce. Lower heat to 250°F and cook 30 minutes more.Serve as is or on rolls.

Pork Loin with Linguine

1 (4- to 6-pound) pork loin roast*

2 teaspoons salt

1 tablespoon black pepper

3 tablespoons extra-virgin olive oil

1 cup *Coca-Cola*®

3 sprigs fresh thyme

2 tablespoons butter

¼ cup sour cream

1 pound linguine, cooked with 1 cup pasta water reserved

Salt and black pepper

PREHEAT oven to 350°F. Season pork with 2 teaspoons salt and 1 tablespoon pepper. Heat oil in large skillet over medium-high heat and brown pork 4 minutes per side.

BAKE pork in skillet, uncovered, 45 minutes to 1 hour, or until pork has reached an internal temperature of 165°F. Remove pork from oven to plate and tent with foil.

PLACE skillet over medium-high heat and bring juices to a boil. Add *Coca-Cola*, thyme and butter. Reduce heat to a simmer and cook 5 to 8 minutes or until reduced**. Turn off heat.

ADD sour cream. Mix in cooked linguine, salt, pepper and pasta water, if sauce is too thick. Slice roast; serve on top of linguine.

Check to see if the pork has solutions or broth added to it. If so, no additional salt is needed in this recipe.

**To reduce is to heat a liquid, usually a sauce, until its volume has been decreased through evaporation. Usually the volume is reduced to one third or one half of the original volume. The results are a more intense flavor and thicker consistency.*

Cherry Pork Medallions with Coca-Cola®

MAKES 4 SERVINGS

1 pound pork tenderloin

1 tablespoon olive oil

1 jar (10 ounces) cherry preserves

¼ cup *Coca-Cola*®

2 tablespoons light corn syrup

¼ teaspoon ground cinnamon

¼ teaspoon ground nutmeg

¼ teaspoon ground cloves

¼ teaspoon salt

SLICE tenderloin into ½-inch-thick medallions. Heat oil in large nonstick skillet over medium heat, add pork and cook about 2 minutes per side. Remove pork from skillet; set aside.

COMBINE cherry preserves, *Coca-Cola*, corn syrup, cinnamon, nutmeg, cloves and salt in same skillet. Bring to a boil over medium-high heat, stirring constantly, about 3 minutes.

RETURN pork to skillet; cover and simmer 8 to 10 minutes or until pork is cooked through.

Note

This recipe uses pork tenderloin with a sweet, savory sauce—perfect for a quick weeknight dish or as an easy weekend meal.

Spicy Pork Po' Boys

MAKES 4 SERVINGS

1 tablespoon paprika

1 tablespoon granulated garlic

1 tablespoon onion powder

2 tablespoons chili powder

1 teaspoon ground red pepper

½ to 1 tablespoon salt

1 tablespoon black pepper

1 pound boneless pork ribs

½ cup *Coca-Cola*®

1 tablespoon hot pepper sauce

Dash Worcestershire sauce

½ cup ketchup

4 French rolls, toasted

½ cup prepared coleslaw

MIX dry ingredients together to create a rub and coat meat well on all sides. Let ribs sit at least 3 hours or overnight.

PLACE meat in covered ceramic dish or Dutch oven. Combine *Coca-Cola*, hot pepper sauce and Worcestershire sauce; drizzle evenly over meat.

BAKE, covered, at 250°F at least 4 hours. (Meat should easily fall apart.)

REMOVE meat from dish or Dutch oven. Add ketchup to sauce in dish and cook 4 to 6 minutes or until sauce has thickened and combined. Pour sauce over meat and break apart with two forks while mixing in sauce.

SERVE pork on toasted French rolls topped with coleslaw.

Tip **Instead of topping with coleslaw, you can also top with shredded lettuce, tomatoes, or pickles.**

Coca-Cola® Ham

½ ham (5 to 6 pounds)

1 cup packed brown sugar

1½ cups *Coca-Cola*®

1 cup crushed pineapple
(optional)

Hamburger rolls

WASH ham thoroughly. Rub fat side with brown sugar.

POUR *Coca-Cola* over ham. Pour crushed pineapple over ham, if desired. Bake at 450°F for 3 hours. Serve on rolls.

Family Pot Roast

3-pound chuck roast, any cut

2 tablespoons oil

1 can (16 ounces) tomatoes, undrained

1 cup *Coca-Cola*®

1 package (1½ ounces) spaghetti sauce mix

1 cup finely cut onion

¾ cup finely cut celery

1½ teaspoons salt

½ teaspoon garlic salt

Cornstarch (optional)

BROWN meat in oil in a Dutch oven, about 10 minutes on each side. Drain off fat.

BREAK up tomatoes in their juice; add tomatoes and remaining ingredients, except cornstarch, to medium bowl, stirring until spaghetti sauce mix is dissolved. Pour over meat. Cover, simmer slowly about 2½ hours or until meat is fork-tender. Thicken gravy with cornstarch, if desired, and serve over sliced meat.

COCA-COLA® HAM

Chinese Pepper Steak

MAKES 6 SERVINGS

1- to 1½-pound boneless top round or sirloin steak

2 tablespoons oil

1 clove garlic, minced

1 teaspoon salt

1 cup canned undiluted beef broth

1 cup thinly sliced green pepper strips

1 cup thinly sliced celery

¼ cup thinly sliced onions

½ cup plus ¼ cup *Coca-Cola®**, divided

2 medium ripe tomatoes

2½ tablespoons cornstarch

1 tablespoon soy sauce

Hot cooked rice

TRIM all fat from meat and cut into pencil-thin strips. In deep skillet or Dutch oven, heat oil, garlic and salt. Add meat and brown over high heat about 10 minutes, stirring occasionally with a fork. Add beef broth, cover and simmer 15 to 20 minutes or until meat is fork-tender. Stir in green pepper, celery, onions and ½ cup *Coca-Cola*.

COVER and simmer 5 minutes. Do not overcook; vegetables should be crisp-tender. Peel tomatoes, cut into wedges, gently stir into meat. Blend cornstarch with remaining ¼ cup *Coca-Cola* and soy sauce. Stir into meat and cook until thickened, about 1 minute, stirring lightly with fork. Serve over hot rice.

*To reduce foam for accurate measurement, use Coca-Cola at room temperature and stir rapidly.

German Sauerbraten

4 pounds boneless beef rump, sirloin tip or round bone chuck

1½ cups vinegar

1 cup *Coca-Cola*®

¾ cup water

3 onions, peeled and sliced

2 stalks celery, sliced

2 carrots, sliced

10 whole black peppercorns

10 whole cloves

3 bay leaves

2 tablespoons sugar

1½ tablespoons salt

All-purpose flour

3 tablespoons oil or shortening

Gravy (recipe follows)

TWO to four days before serving, wipe meat with damp cloth, then place in large resealable food storage bag.

COMBINE remaining ingredients in bowl, except oil and gravy, and pour over meat. Fasten bag tightly and lay flat in 13×9-inch pan. Refrigerate, turning bag each day. (If you like a sour sauerbraten, let meat marinate four days.)

WHEN ready to cook, remove meat (saving marinade) and dry well. Rub surface lightly with flour. Heat oil or shortening in Dutch oven and slowly brown meat well on all sides. Add 1 cup of marinade liquid plus some vegetables and bay leaves. Cover tightly and simmer on surface heat or in a 350°F oven 3 to 4 hours until meat is fork-tender. (If needed, add more marinade during cooking to keep at least ½-inch liquid in Dutch oven.)

REMOVE meat and keep warm until ready to slice. Strain drippings into a large measuring cup; add several ice cubes; let stand a few minutes for fat to separate. Remove fat, then make gravy.

GRAVY

3 cups drippings plus strained marinade

5 tablespoons flour

5 tablespoons gingersnap crumbs

COMBINE above ingredients in Dutch oven, stir and cook about 5 minutes over medium heat until gravy is thickened. Taste for seasonings.

Tip **This German pickled pot roast should be served with its rich, tangy gingersnap gravy to be truly authentic. Plan ahead because it takes days to properly marinate.**

Limelight Steak BBQ

MAKES 2 SERVINGS

**2 large T-bone steaks
(or other select cut suitable
for barbecuing)**

MARINADE

**2 teaspoons seasoning salt
or steak seasoning**

Fresh ground black pepper

**3 tablespoons
Worcestershire sauce**

6 cloves fresh minced garlic

**2 cans (24 ounces)
Coca-Cola®**

USING a fork, pierce each steak several times on both sides and place in shallow glass baking pan. (Do not use stainless steel.)

SPRINKLE steaks with seasoning salt and black pepper. Pour Worcestershire sauce over steaks and add garlic. Turn steaks over to ensure they are well coated with seasonings.

POUR Coca-Cola over steaks to completely cover. Cover pan with plastic wrap. Refrigerate 2 hours, turning steaks after the first hour. Discard marinade and barbecue steak to desired doneness.

Barbecued Ham

MAKES 4 TO 6 SERVINGS

2 pounds ham (chipped)

1 cup ketchup

1 cup Coca-Cola®

1 chopped onion

Hard rolls (optional)

AT your local deli, purchase 2 pounds good quality ham and have it chipped.

COOK ketchup and Coca-Cola with onion in skillet. Cook slowly over medium heat. When it starts to thicken, add chipped ham and cook to desired consistency. Serve on hard rolls, if desired.

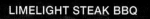
LIMELIGHT STEAK BBQ

Beef Brisket

Center-cut beef brisket

1 packet instant onion soup mix

2 cans (4 ounces each) tomato sauce

Ground ginger

1 bottle (2 liters) Coca-Cola®*, divided

14 to 16 new potatoes

22 to 24 small peeled carrots

PLACE beef brisket in flat roasting pan, fat-side up.

SPRINKLE onion soup mix on top of brisket; pour tomato sauce on top. Sprinkle with ginger. Pour half of 2-liter bottle of *Coca-Cola* over meat.

PLACE whole potatoes and carrots around sides of pan. Add enough water to cover meat.

PLACE in 350°F oven 3½ to 4 hours, occasionally spooning sauce over meat. If necessary, add a little more *Coca-Cola* or water to keep meat covered.

MEAT is done when fork-tender. When finished, remove meat from pan and slice fat cap off top. Using an electric knife, carefully cut meat across grain into ¼-inch slices and place in casserole dish, covering with some of the sauce. Reserve some sauce to be used as gravy.

*Save remaining *Coca-Cola* for another recipe, or serve as a beverage with Beef Brisket.

Tip **Serve with the potatoes, carrots and a fresh loaf of challah (twisted egg bread) for sopping up the gravy.**

Marinated Pork Tenderloin

MAKES 4 TO 6 SERVINGS

1 cup *Coca-Cola*®

¼ cup beef broth

2 tablespoons cider vinegar

1 tablespoon honey mustard

2 small Granny Smith apples, chopped

4 to 6 green onions, finely chopped

2 cloves garlic, minced

1 teaspoon ground cinnamon

½ teaspoon ground ginger

Salt and black pepper

1 to 1½ pounds whole pork tenderloin

COMBINE *Coca-Cola*, beef broth, vinegar and mustard in large bowl; mix well. Add apples, onions, garlic, cinnamon, ginger, salt and pepper to *Coca-Cola* mixture; mix well.

PLACE pork tenderloin in large plastic resealable food storage bag. Pour *Coca-Cola* mixture over pork, turning to coat. Seal bag and marinate in refrigerator at least 3 hours to let flavors blend, turning occasionally.

PREHEAT oven to 350°F. Remove pork from marinade, discard marinade. Place pork in roasting pan. Cook pork about 25 to 30 minutes or until internal temperature reaches 165°F when tested with meat thermometer inserted into thickest part of pork.

REMOVE pork from oven and transfer to cutting board. Let stand 10 to 15 minutes before carving. Internal temperature will continue to rise 5°F to 10°F during stand time. Serve with applesauce and your favorite side dishes.

Matchless Meatloaf

MAKES 4 TO 6 SERVINGS

1½ pounds ground beef

1½ cups fresh bread crumbs

¼ cup minced onion

2 tablespoons finely cut parsley

1 egg

½ cup *Coca-Cola*®

2 tablespoons ketchup

1½ tablespoons prepared mustard

1 teaspoon salt

½ teaspoon basil leaves

⅛ teaspoon black pepper

BREAK up meat with fork in large bowl; add crumbs, onion and parsley, mixing well. Beat egg; mix with remaining ingredients in a separate bowl. Pour over meat mixture. With fork, toss lightly to blend thoroughly. Mixture will be soft.

TURN into a 9×5×3-inch loaf pan. Bake at 350°F for 1 hour. Let set about 10 minutes before slicing.

Coca-Cola® Roast

MAKES 6 SERVINGS

1 beef roast

1 can (12 ounces) *Coca-Cola*®

2 cans cream of mushroom soup

1 package dry onion soup mix

PLACE roast in pan. Mix remaining ingredients together and pour over roast.

COVER tightly with foil and bake at 325°F for about 3 to 4 hours.

MATCHLESS MEATLOAF

Fruited Pork Chops

MAKES 4 SERVINGS

4 rib, loin or shoulder pork chops or smoked pork chops, ½ to ¾ inch thick

1 teaspoon salt

⅛ teaspoon black pepper

⅛ teaspoon ground ginger

1 medium apple

1 medium lemon or orange

2 tablespoons packed brown sugar

½ cup *Coca-Cola*®

1 tablespoon cornstarch

TRIM fat from chops, then brown them on each side in ungreased skillet. Lay chops in shallow baking pan. Do not overlap. Sprinkle with salt, pepper and ginger.

CORE unpeeled apple, cut crosswise into 4 thick slices. Cut lemon into 4 slices; remove seeds. Lay lemon slices atop apple slices and place on each chop.

SPRINKLE with brown sugar. Pour *Coca-Cola* around chops. Cover tightly. Bake in 350°F oven for 45 minutes.

BLEND cornstarch with 2 tablespoons water until smooth. Stir into meat juices. Bake, uncovered, 15 minutes longer or until meat is fork-tender. Spoon sauce over fruit chops to glaze.

Tip **After purchasing pork chops, store them in the coldest part of the refrigerator (on the bottom shelf) for 2 to 3 days. If they are wrapped in butcher paper, they should be rewrapped in plastic wrap to prevent juices from leaking.**

Asian Beef Stir Fry

MAKES 4 SERVINGS

1½ pounds beef flank steak

1 can (12 ounces) *Coca-Cola*®

1 cup beef broth

3 tablespoons soy sauce

1 teaspoon sesame oil

2 cloves garlic, minced

3 tablespoons peanut oil, divided

1 yellow bell pepper, cut into thin strips

1 red bell pepper, cut into thin strips

4 green onions, sliced diagonally

1 cup water chestnuts

1 tablespoon cornstarch

2 cups hot cooked rice

CUT steak in half lengthwise, then crosswise into ⅛-inch strips. Place strips in large resealable food storage bag. Add *Coca-Cola*, beef broth, soy sauce, sesame oil and garlic; seal bag and turn to coat. Marinate at least 3 hours or overnight in refrigerator, turning occasionally.

REMOVE steak from bag; reserve half of marinade in medium bowl. Heat wok or skillet over high heat or until hot. Drizzle 2 tablespoons peanut oil into wok; heat 30 seconds. Add half of steak; stir-fry 2 minutes or until beef is browned and no longer pink. Repeat with remaining steak; set aside.

REDUCE heat to medium-high and add remaining 1 tablespoon peanut oil; heat 30 seconds. Add bell peppers, onions and water chestnuts; cook and stir 3 minutes or until vegetables are tender; remove and set aside.

STIR cornstarch into reserved marinade until smooth. Stir marinade into wok and boil 1 minute, stirring constantly. Return beef and vegetables to wok; cook 3 minutes, or until heated through. Serve over rice.

entrées:
poultry
&seafood

Coca-Cola® Paella

MAKES 4 TO 6 SERVINGS

2 tablespoons extra-virgin olive oil

6 chicken thighs

½ pound hot Italian sausage

1 green bell pepper, cut into strips

1 onion, thinly sliced

1 can (14 ounces) stewed tomatoes, undrained

¾ cup uncooked rice

1 clove garlic, finely chopped

Salt and black pepper

1 can (12 ounces) Coca-Cola®

½ cup frozen peas

½ pound medium shrimp, peeled and deveined

HEAT oil in Dutch oven over medium heat. Brown chicken; remove to plate. Brown sausage, stirring occasionally to break up meat.

ONCE sausage is browned, drain fat and return chicken to pan. Add green peppers and onion and cook and stir until softened. Add tomatoes and their juice, rice, garlic, salt, black pepper and *Coca-Cola*. Increase to high heat and bring to a boil. Once mixture is boiling, reduce heat to low, cover and let simmer 20 minutes.

GENTLY stir in peas and shrimp. Cook an additional 10 minutes. Remove from heat and serve.

Apricot Coca-Cola® and Rosemary Chicken

MAKES 4 SERVINGS

4 boneless skinless chicken breast halves

2 cloves garlic, minced

¼ teaspoon kosher salt

¼ teaspoon red pepper flakes

4 tablespoons apricot preserves

½ cup *Coca-Cola*®

¼ cup low-sodium soy sauce

2 tablespoons chopped fresh rosemary plus additional for garnish

PLACE chicken in large baking dish. Rub garlic, salt and red pepper flakes over chicken. Spread 1 tablespoon apricot preserves over each chicken breast. Drizzle with *Coca-Cola* and soy sauce; sprinkle with 2 tablespoons rosemary. Cover and marinate at room temperature at least 30 minutes.

PREHEAT grill to medium-high heat. Remove chicken from marinade; discard marinade. Grill chicken on lightly greased grill rack coated with cooking spray 5 minutes on each side or until chicken is cooked through. Serve immediately and garnish with fresh rosemary.

Easy Coca-Cola® Chicken

MAKES 4 TO 6 SERVINGS

1 broiler-fryer chicken, cut up into pieces

Salt

1 can (12 ounces) *Coca-Cola*®

1 cup ketchup

CAREFULLY put chicken pieces in electric frying pan. Salt to taste.

COMBINE *Coca-Cola* and ketchup and pour over meat. Cook at 350°F for 1 hour or until done.

APRICOT COCA-COLA® AND ROSEMARY CHICKEN

Sweet and Spicy Shrimp Tacos with Mango Salsa

MAKES 6 SERVINGS

1½ pounds uncooked shrimp, peeled and deveined

1 teaspoon salt

1 teaspoon sugar

½ cup *Coca-Cola®*

⅓ cup chili sauce

2 tablespoons packed brown sugar

1 tablespoon lime juice

1 teaspoon hot pepper sauce

1 tablespoon chopped cilantro

6 lightly grilled flour tortillas

Mango Salsa (recipe follows)

PLACE shrimp in medium bowl and sprinkle with salt and sugar. Stir to coat and refrigerate 30 minutes.

MEANWHILE, heat *Coca-Cola*, chili sauce, brown sugar, lime juice and hot sauce in small skillet over medium heat until sauce begins to simmer and thicken. Remove from heat; stir in cilantro and set aside.

COOK shrimp in large skillet over medium-high heat 3 minutes or until shrimp are pink and opaque.

DRIZZLE sauce over cooked shrimp and serve in flour tortillas topped with Mango Salsa.

MANGO SALSA

2 mangoes, pitted and chopped

1 cucumber, peeled, seeded and chopped

1 red or yellow bell pepper, seeded and chopped

1 jalapeño pepper*, seeded and finely chopped

¼ cup diced red onion

1 clove garlic, minced

2 tablespoons chopped cilantro

1 tablespoon lime juice

1 tablespoon *Coca-Cola®*

Salt and black pepper

COMBINE all ingredients in medium bowl and stir until well combined. Cover and refrigerate 1 to 4 hours before serving.

Jalapeño peppers can sting and irritate the skin, so wear rubber gloves when handling peppers and do not touch your eyes.

Coca-Cola®-Marinated Spanish Chicken

MAKES 4 SERVINGS

1½ pounds bone-in chicken breasts

2 tablespoons dried oregano

2 cloves garlic, minced

½ teaspoon salt

½ teaspoon black pepper

½ cup Spanish green olives with pimientos

⅓ cup capers

1¼ cups *Coca-Cola*®

⅓ cup red wine vinegar

2 tablespoons olive oil

1½ teaspoons paprika

2 tablespoons chopped fresh parsley

PREHEAT oven to 350°F. Season chicken with oregano, garlic, salt and pepper. Place chicken in shallow dish or resealable plastic bag. Add olives and capers.

COMBINE *Coca-Cola*, vinegar and olive oil in small bowl; pour over chicken. Cover and marinate at least 1 hour or up to 8 hours.

ARRANGE chicken mixture in 13×9-inch baking dish and spoon marinade over chicken. Sprinkle both sides of chicken with paprika.

COVER and bake chicken 50 minutes to 1 hour until chicken is cooked through. Serve with additional olives, capers and chopped fresh parsley.

Tip Capers are deep green flower buds of a Mediterranean bush that have been preserved in a vinegary brine. Rinse them in cold water to remove excess salt before using.

Bayou Jambalaya

MAKES 8 SERVINGS

2 large stalks celery, diced

1 onion, diced

28 ounces smoked sausage, cut into ¼-inch slices

3 cloves garlic, chopped

1 red bell pepper, diced

1 tablespoon chopped parsley

1 teaspoon oregano

1 teaspoon thyme

½ teaspoon paprika

½ cup *Coca-Cola*®

½ cup dry white wine

1 can (14 ounces) diced tomatoes, undrained

3 cups water

1 pound uncooked medium shrimp, peeled and deveined

1 bay leaf

1½ cups uncooked long-grain white rice

COMBINE celery, onion and sausage in large skillet over medium-high heat and cook 5 minutes. Add garlic and bell pepper and stir; cook 3 to 4 minutes. Add parsley, oregano, thyme and paprika; stir and cook 1 minute.

ADD *Coca-Cola*, wine, tomatoes and their juice, water, shrimp, bay leaf and rice. Increase to high heat, bring to a boil, then reduce and simmer, covered, 25 minutes or until rice is tender. Remove bay leaf before serving.

Tip **You can make jambalaya with beef, pork, chicken, duck, shrimp, oysters, crayfish, sausage, or any combination.**

Shrimp and Scallop Fettuccine

MAKES 4 TO 6 SERVINGS

1 tablespoon butter

1 small onion, chopped

½ pound sea scallops

½ pound medium shrimp, peeled and deveined

½ pound button mushrooms, sliced

½ cup *Coca-Cola*®

½ cup water

1 tablespoon freshly squeezed lemon juice

3 tablespoons all-purpose flour

1 teaspoon salt

1 cup half-and-half

1 pound spinach fettuccine, cooked

3 tablespoons shredded Parmesan cheese

2 tablespoons chopped fresh parsley

MELT butter in large skillet over medium heat. Add onion; cook until softened and translucent.

ADD scallops, shrimp, mushrooms, *Coca-Cola*, water and lemon juice to skillet. Reduce heat to medium-low. Cover and cook until scallops and shrimp are tender, stirring frequently.

MEANWHILE, blend flour, salt and half-and-half in small bowl. Gradually add flour mixture to seafood mixture, stirring constantly, until thickened and combined.

DIVIDE fettuccine among serving bowls. Spoon seafood mixture over pasta; garnish with Parmesan cheese and parsley.

Note

There are two types of scallops available: sea scallops and bay scallops. Sea scallops are more widely available although they're less tender. Bay scallops are smaller, slightly sweeter, and more expensive.

Creole Shrimp

MAKES 4 TO SERVINGS

2 tablespoons olive oil

½ cup diced green bell pepper

½ cup diced onion

½ cup diced celery

1 teaspoon chili powder

1 can (14 ounces) diced tomatoes, undrained

1 can (8 ounces) tomato sauce

½ cup *Coca-Cola*®

1 tablespoon hot pepper sauce

1 tablespoon Worcestershire sauce

Salt and black pepper

1½ pounds medium shrimp, peeled and deveined

Hot cooked white rice

2 scallions, sliced

HEAT olive oil in stockpot or Dutch oven. Cook and stir bell peppers, onion and celery until soft and translucent. Add chili powder and stir to coat vegetables.

ADD tomatoes and their juice, tomato sauce, *Coca-Cola*, hot pepper sauce, Worcestershire sauce, salt and black pepper. Simmer on low heat, stirring occasionally, until thickened, about 45 minutes.

ADD shrimp to mixture; stir well. Continue simmering 15 minutes. Serve over hot cooked rice and garnish with scallions.

Tip **For a healthier variation, add additional vegetables like zucchini and red bell pepper and serve over brown rice.**

Spice Island Chicken with Pineapple Rice

MAKES 4 SERVINGS

2 tablespoons vegetable oil

1 onion, chopped

2 teaspoons minced fresh garlic

1 teaspoon ground ginger

1 teaspoon five-spice powder

1 cup ketchup

1 can (12 ounces) *Coca-Cola*®

1 can (20 ounces) pineapple chunks in own juice, drained

4 tablespoons soy sauce

2 tablespoons white vinegar

¼ cup packed brown sugar

4 boneless skinless chicken breasts (about 6 ounces each)

2 cups uncooked rice

1 can (8 ounces) crushed pineapple, drained

PREHEAT oven to 350°F. Heat oil In medium saucepan over medium heat. Add onion and cook and stir about 8 minutes until soft and translucent. Stir in garlic, ginger and five-spice powder; cook 1 minute. Add ketchup, *Coca-Cola*, pineapple chunks, soy sauce, vinegar and brown sugar; bring to a boil over medium-high heat until mixture is slightly syrupy, about 15 minutes.

PLACE chicken breasts in greased 13×9-inch baking dish. Cover with pineapple mixture. Bake uncovered, 30 minutes, turning every 10 minutes. Remove from oven, let rest 5 minutes on cutting board before slicing.

MEANWHILE, cook rice. When still hot, toss with crushed pineapple. Place 1 scoop rice on each plate; top with chicken and drizzle with additional pineapple mixture.

Tip For a true "island" flavor, garnish with thinly sliced scallions and cashews.

Country Captain Chicken

MAKES 4 TO 6 SERVINGS

¼ cup olive oil

4 boneless skinless chicken breasts

1 medium onion, sliced

1 medium green bell pepper, sliced

1 can (14½ ounces) chicken broth

1 cup *Coca-Cola*®

1 can (14½ ounces) whole tomatoes, undrained and coarsely chopped

1 can (6 ounces) tomato paste

1 teaspoon hot pepper sauce

½ teaspoon ground white pepper

1 bay leaf

2 tablespoons fresh parsley leaves, chopped

2 cups hot cooked rice

HEAT oil in large skillet over medium-high heat. Add chicken breasts; cook 3 to 4 minutes on each side or until lightly browned. Remove from skillet, set aside.

ADD onion and bell pepper to skillet. Cook and stir 5 minutes or until vegetables are tender. Add chicken broth and *Coca-Cola* to skillet, scraping up any browned bits from bottom of pan. Add tomatoes and their juice, tomato paste, hot pepper sauce, white pepper and bay leaf. Cook and stir 5 minutes or until sauce thickens slightly.

RETURN chicken to pan and simmer, uncovered, about 15 minutes or until chicken is no longer pink in center.

REMOVE chicken breasts to serving platter. Remove bay leaf from sauce. Pour sauce over chicken and garnish with parsley. Serve over rice.

Casserole BBQ Chicken

MAKES 4 TO 6 SERVINGS

3 pounds cut-up chicken or chicken breasts, thighs and legs

⅓ cup all-purpose flour

2 teaspoons salt

⅓ cup oil

½ cup onion, finely diced

½ cup celery, finely diced

½ cup green bell pepper, finely diced

1 cup ketchup

1 cup *Coca-Cola*®*

2 tablespoons Worcestershire sauce

1 tablespoon salt

½ teaspoon hickory smoked salt

½ teaspoon dried basil leaves

½ teaspoon chili powder

⅛ teaspoon black pepper

RINSE chicken pieces; pat dry. Coat chicken with flour and 2 teaspoons salt. Brown pieces on all sides in hot oil, then place pieces in a 3-quart casserole. (Discard drippings.)

COMBINE remaining ingredients, mixing well. Spoon sauce over chicken, covering all pieces. Cover casserole, bake at 350°F about 1¼ hours, or until chicken is fork-tender.

To reduce foam for accurate measurement, use Coca-Cola at room temperature and stir rapidly.

Tip **There is no barbecue sauce needed in this recipe. The combination of *Coca-Cola*® with Worcestershire sauce and seasonings creates a smoky flavor ideal for chicken.**

Seafood Gratin

MAKES 6 SERVINGS

½ pound cooked shrimp

½ pound cooked crabmeat

½ pound cooked sole

½ pound cooked lobster

2 tablespoons butter

2 tablespoons all-purpose flour

¾ cup milk

½ cup grated Parmesan cheese

½ cup *Coca-Cola*®

Bread crumbs

PREHEAT oven to 325°F. Cut seafood into bite-sized pieces; place in greased baking dish.

MELT butter in small saucepan. Add flour, whisking constantly to form a roux. When roux is lightly browned, stir in milk and Parmesan cheese. When mixture is slightly thickened, add *Coca-Cola*.

POUR sauce over seafood and top with bread crumbs. Bake gratin 20 to 25 minutes. Remove from oven to cool slightly before serving.

Hoisin Chicken

MAKES 4 SERVINGS

½ cup *Coca-Cola*®

¼ cup soy sauce

2 tablespoons hoisin sauce

2 cloves garlic, minced

1 teaspoon freshly grated ginger

¼ teaspoon red pepper flakes

1½ pounds boneless skinless chicken cutlets

WHISK together *Coca-Cola*, soy sauce, hoisin sauce, garlic, ginger and red pepper flakes in medium bowl; set aside.

PLACE chicken in large resealable food storage bag. Pour *Coca-Cola* mixture over chicken and cover and refrigerate at least 30 minutes or overnight.

PREHEAT grill to medium-high heat.

REMOVE chicken from marinade; discard marinade. Grill half of chicken on lightly greased grill rack coated with cooking spray 2 to 3 minutes on each side or until chicken is done. Repeat with remaining chicken.

Sweet Southern Barbecue Chicken

MAKES 4 SERVINGS

2 to 3 tablespoons oil, divided

½ cup chopped onion

1 clove garlic, minced

½ cup packed brown sugar

1 teaspoon dry mustard

1 tablespoon honey mustard

1 tablespoon Dijon mustard

1 cup *Coca-Cola*®

2 tablespoons balsamic vinegar

2 tablespoons cider vinegar

2 tablespoons Worcestershire sauce

½ cup ketchup

2 to 3 pounds boneless skinless chicken thighs

SAUCE

HEAT 1 tablespoon oil in medium skillet over medium heat. Add onion and garlic and cook 2 minutes.

ADD next 4 ingredients; bring to a boil over medium-high heat, reduce heat and simmer, uncovered, 20 minutes or until sauce thickens.

ADD *Coca-Cola*, balsamic vinegar, cider vinegar, Worcestershire sauce and ketchup; stir.

SIMMER 15 to 20 minutes, until sauce thickens. Remove from heat.

CHICKEN

HEAT remaining oil in large skillet over medium-high heat. Add half of chicken and cook until cooked through, about 5 to 7 minutes per side. After turning, brush chicken with barbecue sauce. Brush both sides again with sauce in the last 1 to 2 minutes of cooking. Serve chicken with additional sauce. Repeat with remaining chicken.

Teriyaki Chicken

MAKES 4 TO 6 SERVINGS

1 cup soy sauce

½ cup *Coca-Cola*®

2 tablespoons orange juice

1 tablespoon fresh minced ginger

1 clove garlic, minced

Salt, black pepper and chili powder

1 pound boneless skinless chicken breasts, cut into strips

¼ cup vegetable oil

COMBINE first 6 ingredients in small bowl. Place chicken in large resealable food storage bag. Pour marinade over chicken, turning to coat. Seal bag and marinade in refrigerator overnight. Remove chicken from marinade (reserve marinade).

PLACE chicken on well-oiled pan and bake at 350°F about 30 minutes. Remove from oven, slide chicken around in pan to sop up caramelized sauce, baste with reserved marinade and return to oven an additional 15 minutes.

Tip If you have any chicken left over, simply combine it with mixed greens, sliced bell peppers, green onions, and cucumber for a delicious and healthful teriyaki chicken salad.

Seared Scallops with Coca-Cola® Glaze

MAKES 4 SERVINGS

1 tablespoon butter

1¼ pounds sea scallops, rinsed and dried well

2 tablespoons *Coca-Cola*®

1 tablespoon white wine

1 teaspoon soy sauce

1 teaspoon packed brown sugar

HEAT butter in large skillet over medium-high heat. Add scallops and cook 2 to 3 minutes per side, or until scallops are opaque. Remove scallops to plate.

ADD *Coca-Cola*, white wine, soy sauce and brown sugar to skillet; cook 20 to 30 seconds, until liquid thickens. Add scallops and heat through and glaze. Serve immediately.

TERIYAKI CHICKEN

Indian Chicken Curry

MAKES 6 SERVINGS

2½ pounds cut-up chicken or chicken breasts

Celery tops

3 tablespoons butter or margarine

1 tart apple, peeled and diced

1 medium onion, thinly sliced

1 tablespoon curry powder, or to taste

⅓ cup raisins

½ cup *Coca-Cola*®

3½ tablespoons all-purpose flour

1 cup coffee cream or undiluted evaporated milk

1 teaspoon salt

⅛ teaspoon white pepper

Hot cooked rice

RINSE chicken and cook in large pot of boiling salted water with a few celery tops. Cover and simmer about 1 hour or until fork-tender. Drain, saving strained broth, about 1 cup.

REMOVE chicken from bones and cut into ½-inch pieces to measure about 2½ cups. Melt butter in skillet. Add apple, onion and curry powder, if desired, and cook and stir 5 minutes, blending well. Stir in raisins, reserved chicken broth and *Coca-Cola*.

MIX flour with cream, salt and pepper, stirring until smooth. Add to apple/onion mixture. Stir and cook over low heat until thick and creamy. Season to taste.

ADD chicken; place in covered container to chill overnight. Reheat chicken in top of double boiler over hot water and serve on hot cooked rice with a selection of condiments.

Tip Provide a sampling of the following condiments for sprinkling on top of each serving: grated coconut, chopped peanuts, chopped raw onion, raisins, sweet pickle relish, chutney, or lime wedges.

Balsamic Coca-Cola® Chicken

MAKES 4 SERVINGS

½ cup chopped shallots

2 tablespoons olive oil, divided

1 cup *Coca-Cola*®

⅓ cup balsamic vinegar

1½ pounds boneless skinless chicken cutlets

2 cloves garlic, minced

2 tablespoons chopped fresh basil leaves

½ teaspoon salt

½ teaspoon black pepper

Fresh basil leaves (optional)

PREHEAT grill to medium-high heat.

COOK shallots in 1 tablespoon oil in large nonstick skillet over medium heat 3 minutes or until tender. Add *Coca-Cola* and balsamic vinegar and simmer over low heat 10 minutes or until reduced to ⅔ cup. Reserve ¼ cup in separate bowl and set aside.

PLACE chicken on nonstick baking sheet. Rub with garlic, chopped basil, salt and pepper; drizzle with remaining olive oil.

GRILL chicken on a lightly greased grill rack coated with cooking spray 2 to 3 minutes on each side or until chicken is done, basting with reserved ¼ cup *Coca-Cola*/balsamic mixture. Serve immediately with remaining balsamic mixture and garnish with fresh basil, if desired.

Tip **Be sure to use chicken cutlets in this recipe. Chicken cutlets are boneless, skinless sections of the chicken breast which have been tenderized. Cutlets cook quicker than chicken breasts.**

sides, sauces &salads

Coca-Cola® Chutney Carrots

MAKES 4 SERVINGS

2 cups baby carrots

1 can (12 ounces) Coca-Cola®

1 cup water plus additional, as needed

3 tablespoons cranberry chutney

1 tablespoon Dijon mustard

2 teaspoons butter

2 tablespoons chopped pecans, toasted

PLACE carrots in medium saucepan over medium-high heat; cover with Coca-Cola and 1 cup water. Bring to a boil, reduce heat and simmer until carrots are tender, about 8 minutes.

DRAIN carrots and return to saucepan. Add chutney, mustard and butter. Cook and stir over medium-low heat until carrots are glazed.

PLACE carrots in serving bowl. Top with pecans.

Note

Mango chutney can be used in place of cranberry chutney.

Roasted Potato Salad with Vegetables

4 to 5 small red potatoes, cut into 1-inch cubes (about 5 cups)

2 sweet potatoes, cut into 1-inch cubes (about 3 cups)

⅓ cup diced red onion

1 tablespoon plus 1 teaspoon olive oil

2 tablespoons *Coca-Cola®*

2 teaspoons balsamic vinegar

1 tablespoon packed brown sugar

Salt and black pepper

2 cups green beans, cut into 1-inch pieces

2 large tomatoes, seeded and chopped

1 yellow, red or orange bell pepper, chopped

DRESSING

1 tablespoon mayonnaise

3 tablespoons honey mustard

3 tablespoons *Coca-Cola®*

1 teaspoon balsamic vinegar

PREHEAT oven to 400°F. Mix red potatoes, sweet potatoes, onion, olive oil, 2 tablespoons *Coca-Cola* and vinegar on rimmed baking sheet.

SPRINKLE with brown sugar, salt and black pepper and mix to coat. Roast 17 to 20 minutes, until potatoes are browned and tender.

MEANWHILE, steam green beans over boiling water until crisp-tender, about 3 to 4 minutes.

WHEN potatoes and green beans are done, combine with tomatoes and bell peppers. Add dressing and stir until all ingredients are coated. Serve hot or warm.

Trio of Sweet and Spicy Dipping Sauces

MAKES 3 CUPS SAUCE

APRICOT SAUCE

4 tablespoons apricot preserves

½ cup *Coca-Cola*®

¼ cup soy sauce

1 teaspoon red pepper flakes (optional)

MIX preserves, *Coca-Cola*, soy sauce and red pepper flakes, if desired, in small saucepan over medium-low heat. Cook and stir until mixture is warmed and combined.

RASPBERRY CHIPOTLE SAUCE

1 cup fresh raspberries

2 tablespoons sugar

¼ cup *Coca-Cola*®

3 canned whole chipotle chilies in adobo sauce, drained and chopped

COMBINE all ingredients in small saucepan over medium heat. Simmer, stirring occasionally, until sugar dissolves and mixture is thickened and combined.

PURÉE sauce in blender; strain into serving bowl.

GINGER-SOY SAUCE

¼ cup soy sauce

3 tablespoons white vinegar

3 tablespoons *Coca-Cola*®

1 tablespoon chopped fresh ginger

2 teaspoons sugar

2 teaspoons sesame oil

½ teaspoon salt

COMBINE all ingredients in small mixing bowl. Whisk thoroughly to combine.

Tip **Pair these dipping sauces with chicken, vegetable, or shrimp skewers. They make great party appetizers!**

FROM TOP TO BOTTOM,
GINGER-SOY SAUCE,
RASPBERRY CHIPOTLE SAUCE,
APRICOT SAUCE

Asian-Glazed Roasted Asparagus

MAKES 4 SERVINGS

3 tablespoons *Coca-Cola*®, divided

1 tablespoon plus 1 teaspoon soy sauce, divided

1 tablespoon white wine

1 teaspoon packed brown sugar

1 clove garlic, minced

1 teaspoon cornstarch

1 pound asparagus, ends trimmed

1 tablespoon olive oil

Salt and black pepper

Toasted sesame seeds

PREHEAT oven to 375°F. Combine 2 tablespoons *Coca-Cola* and 1 tablespoon soy sauce with white wine, brown sugar, garlic and cornstarch. Set aside.

TOSS asparagus with olive oil, remaining 1 tablespoon *Coca-Cola* and 1 teaspoon soy sauce on rimmed baking sheet, then season with salt and pepper. Bake 10 to 12 minutes, until asparagus is crisp-tender.

HEAT large skillet over medium-high heat. Add asparagus and sauce to pan and stir to coat. When sauce has thickened, remove from heat and serve. Sprinkle with toasted sesame seeds.

Tip **When selecting asparagus, look for firm, smooth green stems with tightly closed tips; tips that are open are a sign of age. Look for even green shading along the whole length; ends that become lighter in color may be a sign of toughness. Avoid wilted spears and asparagus that has a strong odor.**

Thick Barbecue Sauce

MAKES 2 CUPS

2 medium onions

¾ cup *Coca-Cola*®

¾ cup ketchup

2 tablespoons vinegar

2 tablespoons Worcestershire sauce

½ teaspoon chili powder

½ teaspoon salt

SHRED or blender-chop onions. Combine all ingredients in medium saucepan over high heat. Bring to a boil. Cover; reduce heat and simmer about 45 minutes or until sauce is very thick. Stir occasionally.

Tip **Use this recipe on chicken (see page 94), beef, or even tofu.**

Steak-Fried Onions

MAKES 4 SERVINGS

2 medium white onions

Meat drippings (from a piece of meat you have fried or pan drippings from a roasted piece)

⅛ cup *Coca-Cola*®

PEEL and slice onions. Drop sliced onions in meat drippings in medium saucepan over high heat; stir slightly.

ADD *Coca-Cola*. Stir continually until the pan is deglazed and onions are opaque (about 2 to 3 minutes). Remove from pan and serve.

THICK BARBECUE SAUCE

Barbecue Ranch Chicken Salad

MAKES 4 SERVINGS

2 chicken breasts, grilled and cut into strips

½ cup Thick Barbecue Sauce (*recipe page 92*)

1 package mixed salad greens

1 tomato, cut into wedges

½ cup thinly sliced red onion

½ cup canned corn, rinsed and drained

½ cup canned black beans, rinsed and drained

½ cup ranch salad dressing

½ cup shredded Cheddar cheese

TOSS chicken breasts lightly with Thick Barbecue Sauce; set aside.

MIX salad greens, tomato, onion, corn and black beans in medium bowl.

TOP with sliced chicken, drizzle with ranch dressing and Cheddar cheese. Serve with additional barbecue sauce, if desired.

Mushroom Coca-Cola® Gravy

MAKES ABOUT 2 CUPS GRAVY

4 tablespoons vegetable oil

⅓ cup flour

Salt and black pepper

1 cup beef broth

1 cup *Coca-Cola*®

1 tablespoon butter

⅓ cup onion, finely chopped

1 cup fresh mushrooms, sliced

1½ teaspoons garlic, minced

1½ teaspoons chopped fresh parsley

HEAT oil in skillet over medium-high heat; add flour to create a thin roux. Sprinkle mixture with salt and pepper. Stir mixture constantly.

WHEN roux becomes opaque, pour in broth and *Coca-Cola*, whisking constantly to avoid lumps.

CONTINUING to stir, reduce heat to medium-low, and let mixture bubble (do not boil) until thickened, about 5 minutes. Reduce heat further to low, cover pan and simmer 10 minutes. Continue checking on mixture and stirring as needed.

MEANWHILE, melt butter in separate skillet. Add onion, mushrooms, garlic and parsley. Cook and stir until onions are translucent. Add onion mixture to *Coca-Cola* mixture. Bring heat up to medium and simmer until thickened and combined, about 5 minutes.

Tip **Serve with chicken, beef, turkey, or even with pasta.**

Braised Brussels Sprouts with Caramelized Onions

MAKES 4 SERVINGS

½ tablespoon butter

1 cup diced onion

5 tablespoons *Coca-Cola*®, divided

1 teaspoon balsamic vinegar

1 pound Brussels sprouts, trimmed and halved lengthwise

3 tablespoons dry white wine, divided

Salt and black pepper

HEAT butter in large skillet over medium heat. Reduce heat to medium-low and add onion; cook 10 minutes. Add 1 tablespoon *Coca-Cola* and balsamic vinegar, then cook 5 more minutes.

WHILE onions are cooking, steam Brussels sprouts in medium saucepan over boling water, about 5 minutes. Add Brussels sprouts to pan with onions and increase heat to medium. Add 2 tablespoons white wine and 2 tablespoons *Coca-Cola* and cook about 3 minutes, until most of the liquid has evaporated from the pan.

ADD remaining 1 tablespoon wine and 2 tablespoons *Coca-Cola* to pan; stir and cook 2 minutes or until most liquid has evaporated from pan and Brussels sprouts are tender. Season with salt and pepper.

Note

The caramelized onions add a tasty touch to these bright green vegetables.

Uncle Joe's Baked Beans

MAKES 4 SERVINGS

8 slices bacon, cut into ½-inch pieces

1 medium onion, chopped

1 can (12 ounces) *Coca-Cola*®

1 can (6 ounces) tomato paste

1 tablespoon Dijon mustard

1 teaspoon hot pepper sauce

1 can (15 ounces) kidney beans, rinsed and drained

1 can (15 ounces) pinto beans, drained

2 cans (8 ounces each) crushed pineapple, drained

COOK bacon and onion over medium-high heat in large skillet until bacon is browned and crispy. Drain fat; set aside.

PREHEAT oven to 375°F. Spray 11×7-inch baking dish with nonstick cooking spray.

COMBINE *Coca-Cola*, tomato paste, mustard and hot pepper sauce in large bowl; mix well. Add beans, pineapple and bacon mixture to *Coca-Cola* mixture; mix well. Transfer to prepared dish. Bake, uncovered, 20 to 25 minutes or until beans are hot and bubbly.

Tip **Baked beans are a real crowd-pleaser! Serve this party favorite alongside burgers at your next get-together or family gathering!**

Sweet-Sour Cabbage

MAKES 4 SERVINGS

1½ pounds red or green cabbage	COARSELY shred or cut cabbage (should measure 3 cups).
2 medium apples	CORE and dice unpeeled apples. In large saucepan, toss together cabbage, apples and all remaining ingredients.
½ cup *Coca-Cola*®*	
2 tablespoons vinegar	
2 tablespoons packed brown sugar	COVER; simmer until cabbage is tender, about 25 minutes. Stir occasionally. Serve.
2 tablespoons bacon drippings	*To reduce foam for accurate measurement, use Coca-Cola at room temperature and stir rapidly.*
1 teaspoon salt	
½ to 1 teaspoon caraway seeds	

Coca-Cola® Mashed Sweet Potatoes

MAKES 4 SERVINGS

2 large sweet potatoes, peeled and cubed	COOK potatoes in salted boiling water until tender, about 20 minutes.
¼ cup *Coca-Cola*®	DRAIN completely and add *Coca-Cola* and butter, then mash.
3 tablespoons butter	STIR in nutmeg, salt and pepper.
¼ teaspoon ground nutmeg	
Salt and black pepper	

SWEET-SOUR CABBAGE

Grecian Green Beans

MAKES 4 TO 6 SERVINGS

2 cans (16 ounces each) small whole green beans

2 shallots

2 cloves garlic, minced

¼ cup chopped parsley

2 tablespoons sugar

2 teaspoons oregano

2 teaspoons prepared mustard

½ teaspoon salt

½ cup *Coca-Cola*®

¼ cup olive oil

2 tablespoons vinegar

DRAIN beans and discard liquid. Peel and thinly slice shallots; separate into rings. In large bowl, combine garlic with remaining ingredients, stirring until sugar is dissolved.

ADD beans and shallots; toss lightly with fork. Pack into 1-quart glass jar. Cover and refrigerate several hours or overnight for flavors to blend.

Tip **Serve chilled or as a hot vegetable with steak, hamburger, or meat loaf. Made ahead and refrigerated, this tangy dish does double-duty as a hot vegetable or cold salad and relish.**

Grilled Romaine Hearts with Tangy Vinaigrette

MAKES 6 SERVINGS

TANGY VINAIGRETTE

3 cups *Coca-Cola*®

⅓ cup white vinegar

⅓ cup canola oil

¼ cup sugar

1 teaspoon salt

½ teaspoon onion powder

½ teaspoon garlic powder

3 tablespoons ketchup

1 tablespoon balsamic vinegar

⅛ teaspoon black pepper

2 tablespoons honey mustard

GRILLED ROMAINE HEARTS

4 romaine hearts

¼ to ½ cup olive oil

Salt and black pepper

COMBINE *Coca-Cola*, white vinegar, canola oil, sugar, 1 teaspoon salt, onion powder, garlic powder, ketchup, balsamic vinegar, ⅛ teaspoon pepper and mustard in medium bowl; set aside.

PREPARE grill for direct cooking (medium-high heat). Cut romaine hearts in half lengthwise, drizzle with olive oil and sprinkle generously with salt and pepper.

GRILL about 2 minutes on both sides, until lightly charred and wilted.

DRIZZLE with Tangy Vinaigrette and serve.

Mustard Herb Dressing

MAKES 1¾ CUPS

1 cup olive oil	COMBINE all ingredients in small mixing bowl. Beat until well blended.
½ cup *Coca-Cola*®	
¼ cup wine, cider vinegar or lemon juice	POUR into covered glass jar. Chill several hours to blend flavors. Shake before using.
1 tablespoon Dijon mustard	
1½ teaspoons Italian seasoning	
1 teaspoon salt	
½ small clove garlic, minced	

Tip **This sweet-sour Italian-style dressing keeps very well and can be used on vegetable or fruit salads.**

Southern Caramelized Vidalias

MAKES 4 SERVINGS

2 cups *Coca-Cola*®	BRING *Coca-Cola* and onion to a boil over medium-high heat in large skillet. Boil uncovered, 23 to 25 minutes, or until all liquid is evaporated and onion is richly glazed and browned, stirring occasionally.
1 large yellow onion cut into ½-inch wedges, layers separated	
1 to 2 teaspoons steak sauce	
¼ teaspoon salt	REMOVE from heat, stir in steak sauce, salt, black pepper and red pepper flakes, if desired. Let stand 5 minutes to absorb flavors.
¼ teaspoon black pepper	
⅛ teaspoon red pepper flakes (optional)	

MUSTARD HERB DRESSING

Creamy Caribbean Shrimp Salad

MAKES 4 SERVINGS

1 cup mayonnaise

¼ cup cocktail sauce

¼ cup *Coca-Cola*®

1 teaspoon lime juice

½ teaspoon salt

¼ teaspoon black pepper

1 pound shrimp, cooked and cleaned

1 package (10 ounces) prepared mixed salad greens

2 ripe mangoes, peeled, pitted and sliced

½ cup chopped walnuts

COMBINE mayonnaise, cocktail sauce, *Coca-Cola*, lime juice, salt and pepper in small jar with tight-fitting lid. Shake well. Refrigerate until ready to use.

COMBINE shrimp, salad greens, mangoes and walnuts in large bowl. Divide mixture onto plates. Drizzle dressing over salads.

Tip **The unique flavors of this salad make it an out-of-the-ordinary treat for your next gathering. For an extra-special flavor, try grilling the shrimp before adding it to the salad.**

Sichuan Green Beans with Mushrooms

MAKES 4 SERVINGS

2 tablespoons soy sauce

2 tablespoons *Coca-Cola*®

1 teaspoon sugar

1 tablespoon honey mustard

1 teaspoon cornstarch

3 tablespoons oil, divided

1 pound green beans

8 ounces white button or shiitake mushrooms

3 cloves garlic

1 teaspoon chopped fresh ginger

MIX soy sauce, *Coca-Cola*, sugar, mustard and cornstarch in small bowl and set aside.

HEAT 2 tablespoons oil in 12-inch skillet over medium-high heat. Add green beans and stir-fry 8 to 10 minutes, until beans are crisp-tender and their skins are browned and shriveled. Transfer beans to a bowl or plate.

HEAT remaining 1 tablespoon oil to skillet. Add mushrooms and cook until tender, 2 to 3 minutes for button mushrooms or 4 to 5 for shiitakes. Add garlic and ginger and cook 30 seconds.

RETURN beans to skillet with mushrooms and add sauce. Sauce will thicken immediately; stir until beans are heated through.

Japanese Pickled Cauliflower

MAKES 4 TO 6 SERVINGS

1 medium-sized head cauliflower

1 green bell pepper

½ cup very thinly sliced celery

¾ cup *Coca-Cola*®

6 tablespoons wine vinegar or white vinegar

¼ cup sugar

1½ teaspoons salt

BREAK off each floweret of cauliflower, wash and drain. Wash and remove seeds from green pepper; cut into thin 2-inch strips.

COMBINE cauliflower and green pepper in large bowl. Cover with boiling water; let stand 2 minutes; drain thoroughly. Add celery.

HEAT *Coca-Cola* with remaining ingredients in small saucepan. Pour over vegetables. Toss lightly with a fork, and pack into a 1-quart glass jar. Push down lightly so liquid covers vegetables. Cover and chill overnight.

Tip **A delicately flavored, crisp relish or salad to serve with sandwiches, hamburgers, meat loaf, or barbecued chicken.**

desserts

Chocolate Coca-Cola® Cupcakes with Cherries

MAKES 27 CUPCAKES

1 package dark chocolate cake mix

Eggs and oil, per cake mix instructions

1 can *Coca-Cola*®

1 jar (8 ounces) maraschino cherries in syrup

1 can (21 ounces) cherry pie filling, lightly drained

Cherry Butter Cream Frosting (recipe follows)

PREPARE cake mix according to package directions, substituting *Coca-Cola* for water.

ADD maraschino cherry syrup and cherry pie filling.

LINE muffin cups with paper baking cups. Pour batter into cups and bake according to directions for cupcakes.

COOL completely; frost with Cherry Butter Cream frosting and top each with a maraschino cherry.

CHERRY BUTTER CREAM FROSTING

5½ tablespoons butter, softened

2 tablespoons cream cheese, softened

2½ cups confectioners sugar

2 tablespoons maraschino cherry syrup

USING an electric mixer, beat together butter, cream cheese and sugar in medium bowl until fluffy, about 1 minute.

ADD cherry syrup and beat until combined and creamy.

Coca-Cola® and Chocolate S'mores

MAKES 8 SERVINGS

¼ cup butter or margarine

3 tablespoons *Coca-Cola*®

2 tablespoons cocoa

1⅓ cups confectioners sugar

½ teaspoon vanilla extract

8 graham crackers, broken in half (16 squares)

2 milk chocolate bars, broken into individual squares

1 cup mini marshmallows

PREHEAT oven to broil. Heat butter, *Coca-Cola* and cocoa over medium-low heat in small saucepan, stirring until butter melts. Remove from heat and whisk in confectioners sugar and vanilla. Set aside.

PLACE graham crackers on foil-lined baking sheet. Top each graham cracker with 1 individual chocolate square. Drizzle 1 teaspoon chocolate/*Coca-Cola* mixture over each chocolate square and sprinkle marshmallows evenly over the top. Place baking sheet in preheated oven 1 minute or until marshmallows are golden brown and puff up.

REMOVE from oven and place remaining graham cracker square halves on top of marshmallows, pressing together gently.

Note

You may also grill s'mores over indirect medium heat 2 minutes or until chocolate melts and marshmallows are roasted.

Coca-Cola® Float Cupcakes

MAKES 18 CUPCAKES

1 box vanilla cake mix

Eggs and oil, per cake mix instructions

1 can *Coca-Cola*®

Coca-Cola® Buttercream (recipe follows)

Vanilla Buttercream (recipe follows)

Maraschino cherries

PREPARE cake mix according to package directions, substituting *Coca-Cola* for water.

LINE 24 standard muffin cups with paper baking cups. Pour batter into prepared muffin cups and bake according to cake mix directions.

ALLOW cupcakes to cool completely on wire rack.

FROST with *Coca-Cola*® Buttercream; top with Vanilla Buttercream and garnish with maraschino cherry.

COCA-COLA® BUTTERCREAM

½ cup (1 stick) butter, softened

1½ cups confectioners sugar

2 tablespoons *Coca-Cola,* plus additional as needed

BEAT butter and confectioners sugar in large bowl until smooth.

STIR in *Coca-Cola*, adding additional *Coca-Cola* in small drops, if necessary, until frosting is creamy and spreadable.

VANILLA BUTTERCREAM

5½ tablespoons butter, softened

2½ cups confectioners sugar

2 teaspoons vanilla extract

1 tablespoon milk

BEAT butter and sugar in large bowl until smooth.

STIR in vanilla and milk until smooth.

Coca-Cola® Pecan Pie

MAKES 8 TO 10 SERVINGS

1 package (15 ounces) refrigerated pie crust

3 eggs

¾ cup sugar

½ cup corn syrup

¼ cup *Coca-Cola®*

2 tablespoons butter or margarine, melted

1½ teaspoons vanilla extract

¼ teaspoon salt

1½ cups pecan halves

Vanilla ice cream (optional)

PREHEAT oven to 350°F. Unroll 1 pie crust and place in 9-inch pie plate. Unroll remaining crust and press over bottom crust; gently press crusts together. Fold edges under and crimp.

STIR together eggs, sugar, corn syrup, *Coca-Cola*, butter, vanilla and salt in large bowl; stir in pecans. Pour filling into pie crust. Bake 55 minutes or until set. Serve warm or cold with ice cream, if desired.

Tip **Your kitchen will be filled with heavenly aromas when you make this family-favorite classic pie.**

Mocha Coca-Cola® Float

MAKES 4 SERVINGS

1 cup coffee ice cream

1 cup vanilla ice cream

2 cups *Coca-Cola*®

1 cup whipped cream

4 teaspoons miniature chocolate chips

SCOOP ¼ cup coffee ice cream and ¼ cup vanilla ice cream into 4 tall, chilled glasses. Slowly pour in ½ cup *Coca-Cola* into each glass. Top each evenly with whipped cream and chocolate chips. Serve with straw and long spoon.

Note

Does it matter if you add the ice cream or the soda first? Adding the ice cream first prevents splashing and overflowing!

Cuba Libre Chiffon Pie

MAKES 1 (9-INCH) PIE

1 cup sugar, divided

1 envelope (1 tablespoon) unflavored gelatin

⅛ teaspoon salt

1 cup *Coca-Cola*®

3 eggs, separated

¼ cup fresh lime juice

¼ cup dark rum

1 cup whipped topping or whipped cream

1 9-inch graham cracker or chocolate cookie crust or baked pie shell

2 tablespoons grated lime peel

STIR together ½ cup sugar, gelatin and salt in top of double boiler. Stir in *Coca-Cola*. Beat egg yolks; stir into *Coca-Cola* mixture. Cook over boiling water, stirring constantly, until gelatin is dissolved, about 5 minutes.

REMOVE from boiling water; stir in lime juice and rum. Chill until mixture mounds when dropped from spoon. Beat egg whites until soft peaks form. Gradually beat in remaining ½ cup sugar; beating until stiff and glossy. Fold gelatin mixture into whipped topping, then carefully fold this into egg whites. Chill several minutes then pile into pie crust.

SPRINKLE with grated peel. Chill several hours until firm. If desired, top with dollop of whipped cream.

MOCHA COCA-COLA® FLOAT

Fudgey Coca-Cola® Brownies

MAKES 16 SERVINGS

4 unsweetened chocolate baking squares (1 ounce each)

½ cup butter or margarine

1 cup granulated sugar

¾ cup firmly packed dark brown sugar

2 eggs

2 tablespoons *Coca-Cola*®

1 cup all-purpose flour

1 teaspoon vanilla extract

Coca-Cola® Frosting (recipe follows)

PREHEAT oven to 350°F. Line bottom and sides of 8-inch pan with aluminum foil; lightly grease foil.

MICROWAVE chocolate squares and butter in a large microwave-safe bowl at HIGH 1½ to 2 minutes or until melted and smooth, stirring at 30-second intervals. Whisk in granulated and brown sugars. Add eggs, 1 at a time, whisking just until blended after each addition. Whisk in *Coca-Cola*, flour and vanilla. Pour mixture into prepared pan.

BAKE at 350°F 40 to 45 minutes or until a wooden pick inserted into center comes out clean. Cool completely on a wire rack and cut brownies into 16 squares. Top with frosting.

COCA-COLA® FROSTING

¼	cup butter or margarine
3	tablespoons *Coca-Cola*®
2	tablespoons cocoa
1⅓	cups confectioners sugar, sifted
½	teaspoon vanilla extract

HEAT butter, *Coca-Cola* and cocoa in medium saucepan over medium-low heat, stirring until butter melts. Remove from heat and whisk in confectioners sugar and vanilla. Set aside.

Coca-Cola® Cake

2 cups sugar	PREHEAT oven to 350°F. Sift sugar and flour in a medium bowl. Add marshmallows. In saucepan, mix butter, oil, cocoa and *Coca-Cola*. Bring to a boil and pour over dry ingredients; blend well. Dissolve baking soda in buttermilk just before adding to batter along with eggs and vanilla, mixing well.
2 cups all-purpose flour	
1½ cups mini marshmallows	
½ cup butter or margarine	
½ cup vegetable oil	
3 tablespoons cocoa	
1 cup *Coca-Cola*®	POUR into a well-greased 13×9-inch pan and bake 35 to 45 minutes. Remove from oven and frost immediately.
1 teaspoon baking soda	
½ cup buttermilk	
2 eggs	**FROSTING**
1 teaspoon vanilla extract	
Frosting (recipe follows)	

FROSTING

½ cup butter

3 tablespoons cocoa

6 tablespoons *Coca-Cola*®

1 box (16 ounces) confectioners sugar

1 teaspoon vanilla extract

1 cup chopped pecans

COMBINE butter, cocoa and *Coca-Cola* in a saucepan. Bring to a boil and pour over confectioners sugar, blending well.

ADD vanilla and pecans. Spread over hot cake. When cool, cut into squares and serve.

Coca-Cola® Carrot Cupcakes

MAKES 12 CUPCAKES

3 eggs

½ cup plus 2 tablespoons oil

¼ cup plus 2 tablespoons Coca-Cola®

½ cup granulated sugar

¼ cup packed brown sugar

1½ cups all-purpose flour

1 teaspoon baking soda

1 teaspoon baking powder

1 teaspoon ground cinnamon

½ teaspoon ground cloves

½ teaspoon ground nutmeg

½ teaspoon salt

½ teaspoon ground ginger

¾ cup grated carrots

Cream Cheese Icing (recipe follows)

PREHEAT oven to 350°F. Combine eggs, oil, Coca-Cola, granulated and brown sugars in large mixing bowl and blend until smooth.

ADD all dry ingredients to bowl and stir until well combined.

STIR in carrots and mix to combine. Pour about ¼ cup batter into 12 paper-lined or greased muffin cups. Bake 15 minutes or until knife inserted into centers of cupcakes comes out clean.

LET cool completely; frost with Cream Cheese Icing.

CREAM CHEESE ICING

1 package cream cheese or Neufchâtel, softened

1¼ cups confectioners sugar

1 tablespoon milk, or as needed

BEAT cream cheese and sugar until light and creamy; add milk as needed to adjust consistency.

Date-Nut Bread

1 package (8 ounces) pitted dates

1¼ cups *Coca-Cola*®

1 cup firmly packed light brown sugar

2 tablespoons oil

2 cups all-purpose flour

1 teaspoon baking powder

1 teaspoon baking soda

1 egg, beaten

1 teaspoon vanilla extract

½ cup chopped pecans or walnuts

CHOP dates. Heat *Coca-Cola* to boiling. Remove from heat and stir in dates, mixing very well.

STIR in brown sugar and oil. Let cool while preparing other ingredients. Lightly spoon flour into cup to measure. Stir together flour, baking powder and baking soda. Add to dates, mixing thoroughly. Stir in egg, vanilla and nuts.

POUR into greased and floured 9×5×3-inch loaf pan. Bake in 350°F oven about 1 hour or until toothpick inserted into center comes out clean. Cool in pan, set on rack, 20 minutes.

REMOVE loaf from pan, set on rack, top side up. When cold, wrap and store overnight before slicing.

Tip An easy, hand-mixed quick bread. The moist, fruity slices make delicious cream cheese sandwiches.

Chocolate Coca-Cola® Cake

MAKES 12 SERVINGS

1 package (18½ ounces) devil's food cake mix*

1 bottle (16 ounces) *Coca-Cola*®, divided

2 tablespoons grated orange peel, divided

½ cup semisweet chocolate chips

12 large fresh, ripe strawberries, preferably unhulled

½ cup butter or margarine, softened

1 package (16 ounces) confectioners sugar

3 tablespoons powdered chocolate drink mix

1½ teaspoons vanilla extract

HEAT oven to 350°F; grease 13×9×2-inch baking pan. Prepare cake mix according to package directions, using 1⅓ cups *Coca-Cola* in place of water and stirring 1 tablespoon grated orange peel in batter. Pour batter into prepared pan.

BAKE 30 minutes or until wooden pick inserted into center comes out clean. Invert cake onto wire rack to cool completely. Cake may be made and stored, tightly wrapped, up to 2 days before decorating.

STIR chocolate chips in small heavy saucepan over very low heat until melted and smooth; remove from heat. Dip strawberries into chocolate to coat halfway, placing each berry as it is dipped on cookie sheet lined with waxed paper. Refrigerate berries until ready to use.

CUT cooled cake horizontally into 2 equal layers with sharp serrated knife; place bottom layer on large cookie sheet.

BEAT butter in large bowl with mixer at medium speed until light and fluffy; gradually beat in confectioners sugar and chocolate drink mix until smooth. Beat in ⅓ cup of remaining *Coca-Cola*, remaining 1 tablespoon grated orange peel and vanilla until thoroughly blended and smooth. Spread half of frosting over bottom cake layer; top with second layer. Swirl remaining frosting over top of cake. Cut cake into 12 portions; arrange on platter. Decorate with chocolate-dipped strawberries and birthday candles, if desired.

For firmer cake, use 1 (16-ounce) package of pound cake mix, stirring in ⅓ cup powdered chocolate drink mix along with grated orange peel. Use Coca-Cola for the liquid; bake as directed.

Molten Lava Coca-Cola® Cakes

MAKES 5 CAKES

5 ounces 60% bittersweet chocolate, chopped

1 tablespoon butter

4 tablespoons heavy cream

2 eggs plus 1 egg yolk

2 tablespoons *Coca-Cola*®

¼ cup oil

1 package (about 10 ounces) brownie mix

Confectioners sugar (optional)

Whipped cream (optional)

PREHEAT oven to 400°F. Melt chocolate in small saucepan with butter; remove from heat and stir in heavy cream.

BEAT 2 eggs and 1 egg yolk 1 minute until frothy. Add *Coca-Cola* and oil. Beat in brownie mix and melted chocolate mixture.

PLACE 5 (3-ounce) greased ramekins on baking sheet. Pour about ½ cup batter into ramekins; bake 14 to16 minutes or until outside edges are set. Cool 3 to 4 minutes.

TO serve, loosen edges of cake from ramekins by using a knife along edges to invert onto plate. Top with confectioners sugar and whipped cream, if desired.

Tip **No one will be able to resist these tempting cakes with their melted sweet fillings.**

Brazilian Iced Chocolate

MAKES 4 TO 6 SERVINGS

2 squares (1 ounce each) unsweetened chocolate

¼ cup sugar

1 cup double strength hot coffee

2½ cups milk

1½ cups *Coca-Cola®*, chilled

Ice cream or whipped cream

MELT chocolate in top of double boiler over hot water. Stir in sugar. Gradually stir in hot coffee, mixing thoroughly.

ADD milk and continue cooking until all particles of chocolate are dissolved and mixture is smooth, about 10 minutes. Pour into jar, cover and chill. When ready to serve, stir in chilled *Coca-Cola*. Serve over ice cubes in tall glasses. Top with ice cream or whipped cream.

Tip **To put a twist on this tasty dessert, try it with different flavors of ice cream, chopped nuts, or caramel sauce.**

Southern Belle Salad

MAKES 7 SERVINGS

1 can (16 ounces) pitted dark sweet cherries

1 package (3 ounces) cherry gelatin

1 cup *Coca-Cola®*

2 tablespoons fresh lemon juice

1 package (3 ounces) cream cheese

½ cup cut-up pecans or walnuts

DRAIN cherry juice. Bring ¾ cup of juice to a boil; add to gelatin. Stir until dissolved.

STIR in *Coca-Cola* and lemon juice. Chill until gelatin mounds slightly.

CUT cream cheese into very small pieces. Fold cream cheese, nuts and whole cherries into gelatin. Spoon into 7 individual molds. Chill until firm.

BRAZILIAN ICED CHOCOLATE

Fresh Banana Cake
with Seafoam Frosting

MAKES 6 SERVINGS

CAKE

1 package (18½ ounces)
yellow cake mix*

⅛ teaspoon baking soda

2 eggs

¾ cup *Coca-Cola®*

1 cup (2 to 3) mashed ripe
bananas

2 teaspoons lemon juice

⅓ cup finely chopped nuts

Sea Foam Frosting
(recipe follows)

SEAFOAM FROSTING

2 egg whites

1½ cups firmly packed light
brown sugar

⅛ teaspoon cream of tartar

⅓ cup *Coca-Cola®*

Dash salt

1 teaspoon vanilla extract

FOR cake, combine mix, baking soda and eggs in large mixing bowl.

MEASURE *Coca-Cola*; stir briskly until foaming stops, and add to batter. Blend ingredients just until moistened, then beat at high speed of electric mixer 3 minutes, scraping bowl often.

COMBINE mashed bananas with lemon juice. Add to cake batter with nuts. Beat 1 minute at medium speed and turn into a generously greased and lightly floured 13×9×2-inch pan.

BAKE at 350°F about 40 minutes or until cake tests done. Cool on rack 15 minutes, remove cake from pan and turn right side up on rack to finish cooling.

FOR frosting, combine all ingredients except vanilla in top of double boiler; beat 1 minute at high speed with electric mixer. Place over boiling water (water should not touch bottom of top part); beat on high speed about 7 minutes or until frosting forms peaks when beater is raised.

REMOVE from boiling water (for smoothest frosting, empty into large bowl). Add vanilla and continue beating on high speed until thick enough to spread, about 2 minutes. Spread on sides and top of cooled banana cake.

Do not use mix with pudding added or one that requires oil.

Coca-Cola® Cherry Salad

MAKES 8 SERVINGS

1 can cherry pie filling

½ cup water

1 large package of cherry gelatin mix

1 can (7½ ounces) crushed pineapple, undrained

1 can (12 ounces) Coca-Cola®

½ cup chopped nuts

1 tub chilled whipped topping

3 ounces cream cheese

BRING pie filling and water to a boil in a medium saucepan over high heat. Remove from heat; add gelatin mix. Stir until mixed.

ADD undrained pineapple and Coca-Cola; stir to combine.

STIR in nuts; refrigerate until set.

MEANWHILE, mix together whipped topping and cream cheese. Spread or dollop over cooled and set salad. Serve.

Tip **Coca-Cola® combines well with the cherry flavor to make a refreshing dessert or sweet side dish.**

Coconut Shake

MAKES 1 TO 2 SERVINGS

1 package coconut pudding

2 cups milk

1½ cups Coca-Cola®

1 package peanuts (medium size)

PREPARE coconut pudding according to package directions. Refrigerate 10 minutes.

COMBINE milk, pudding and Coca-Cola in large bowl. Mix together and gradually add peanuts. Let stand 2 minutes, and then mix in a blender. Let stand again 10 minutes in the refrigerator.

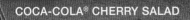
COCA-COLA® CHERRY SALAD

Chocolate Coca-Cola®
Cake with Chocolate
Cream Cheese Frosting

MAKES 1 CAKE

1 box (18¼ ounces) chocolate cake mix

1 cup *Coca-Cola*®

¼ cup water

½ cup oil

3 eggs

Chocolate Cream Cheese Frosting (recipe follows)

CHOCOLATE CREAM CHEESE FROSTING

4 cups confectioners sugar, sifted

⅓ cup unsweetened cocoa powder

1 package (8 ounces) cream cheese, softened

½ cup (1 stick) butter, softened

1 teaspoon vanilla extract

PREHEAT oven to 350°F. Grease 2 (8-inch) round cake pans; set aside.

COMBINE cake mix, *Coca-Cola*, water, oil and eggs in large bowl. Beat at low speed of electric mixer until blended; beat at medium speed 2 minutes. Divide batter between prepared pans.

BAKE 30 to 35 minutes or until toothpick inserted into center of cakes comes out clean. Cool in pans on wire racks 10 minutes. Remove from pans to wire racks; cool completely.

MEANWHILE, prepare Chocolate Cream Cheese Frosting. Combine sifted confectioners sugar and cocoa in large bowl; set aside.

BEAT cream cheese, butter and vanilla in large bowl until smooth. Gradually fold in confectioners sugar and cocoa.

PLACE 1 cake layer on serving plate and frost top and sides with Chocolate Cream Cheese Frosting. Repeat with second layer.

Mixed Fruit Compote

MAKES 6 SERVINGS

1 cup *Coca-Cola*®

1 cup water

¾ cup orange juice

½ teaspoon almond extract

1 can (21 ounces) cherry
pie filling

1 can (16 ounces) sliced
peaches, drained

1 cup dried cranberries

Mint leaves (optional)

COMBINE *Coca-Cola*, water, orange juice and almond extract in large saucepan; mix well. Add pie filling, peaches and cranberries to *Coca-Cola* mixture.

BRING fruit mixture to a boil over medium-high heat. Reduce temperature to low and simmer 12 to 15 minutes or until fruit is tender. Serve warm, at room temperature or chilled. Garnish with mint leaves, if desired.

Note

A compote is a combination of fruits, usually cooked in a light syrup, served for dessert or breakfast. They're usually chilled, but are also wonderful served warm or at room temperature.

Gingerbread Deluxe

MAKES 4 TO 6 SERVINGS

1 package (14 ounces) gingerbread mix

1 tablespoon instant coffee

1 tablespoon grated orange peel

¼ cup orange juice

¾ cup *Coca-Cola*®

COMBINE all ingredients. Beat vigorously with spoon until very well blended, about 1½ minutes.

POUR into 8×8×2-inch greased and floured pan. Bake in 350°F oven 30 to 35 minutes or until center springs back when lightly touched.

COOL 10 minutes; remove from pan and set on rack. Serve as a hot bread or as a dessert with whipped topping.

Scottish Oaten Bread

MAKES 1 LOAF

2 cups all-purpose flour

1 cup old-fashioned rolled oats

½ cup sugar

2½ teaspoons baking powder

½ teaspoon baking soda

1 teaspoon salt

1 egg

3 tablespoons oil or melted shortening

½ teaspoon vanilla extract

1 cup *Coca-Cola*®

1 cup coarsely cut cooked prunes*

½ cup chopped walnuts

LIGHTLY spoon flour into measuring cup; level off. In large bowl, stir together flour, rolled oats, sugar, baking powder, baking soda and salt. With fork, beat egg with oil and vanilla until well blended and stir into flour mixture. Add *Coca-Cola*, very well-drained prunes and nuts; blend thoroughly with spoon.

TURN into generously greased and lightly floured 9×5×3-inch loaf pan. If desired, garnish with prune halves. Bake at 350°F about 1 hour or until toothpick inserted into center comes out clean.

COOL on rack 20 minutes before removing bread from pan. Store in foil overnight before slicing.

*½ lb. dried prunes = 1 cup cut-up cooked prunes.

Tip This moist and fruity quick bread is delicious as is, toasted, or spread with cream cheese for sandwiches.

GINGERBREAD DELUXE

Cherry and Coca-Cola® Apple Rings

MAKES 4 SERVINGS

3 Granny Smith or other tart apples, peeled and cored

½ teaspoon plus ¼ teaspoon sugar-free, cherry-flavored gelatin powder

⅓ cup *Coca-Cola*®

⅓ cup nondairy whipped topping

SLICE apples crosswise into ¼-inch-thick rings; remove seeds. Place stacks of apple rings in large microwavable bowl; sprinkle with gelatin. Pour *Coca-Cola* over rings.

COVER loosely with waxed paper. Microwave on HIGH 5 minutes or until liquid is boiling. Allow to stand, covered, 5 minutes. Arrange on dessert plates. Serve warm with whipped topping.

Tip **You may also use Jonathan apples in this recipe, or a combination of both Granny Smith and Jonathans. They're both good choices for baking and for eating raw.**

Coca-Cola® Peach Float

MAKES 1 SERVING

2 to 3 scoops vanilla ice cream

2 scoops peach yogurt

2 to 3 ounces *Coca-Cola*® (part of 1 can)

SPOON 2 or 3 scoops vanilla ice cream into a small bowl.

ADD peach yogurt.

POUR a few ounces of *Coca-Cola* over the above.

CHERRY AND COCA-COLA® APPLE RINGS

Aloha Burgers with Pineapple Chutney 34

Apricot Coca-Cola® and Rosemary Chicken 62

Asian Beef Stir Fry 58

Asian-Glazed Roasted Asparagus 90

Balsamic Coca-Cola® Chicken 83

Barbecue Ranch Chicken Salad 94

Barbecued Ham 48

Bayou Jambalaya 68

Beef Brisket 50

Black Bean Dip 14

Braised Brussels Sprouts with Caramelized Onions 97

Brazilian Iced Chocolate 128

Caprese Bruschetta 16

Casserole BBQ Chicken 76

Cherry and Coca-Cola® Apple Rings 140

Cherry Pork Medallions with Coca-Cola® 41

Chinese Pepper Steak 46

Chocolate Coca-Cola® Cake 126

Chocolate Coca-Cola® Cake with Chocolate Cream Cheese Frosting 134

Chocolate Coca-Cola® Cupcakes with Cherries 110

Coca-Cola® and Chocolate S'mores 112

Coca-Cola® Cake 121

Coca-Cola® Carrot Cupcakes 122

Coca-Cola® Cherry Salad 132

Coca-Cola® Chili 20

Coca-Cola® Chutney Carrots 84

Coca-Cola® Float Cupcakes 114

Coca-Cola®-Glazed Bacon-Wrapped Dates 24

Coca-Cola® Ham 44

Coca-Cola®-Marinated Spanish Chicken 66

Coca-Cola® Mashed Sweet Potatoes 100

Coca-Cola® Paella 60

Coca-Cola® Peach Float 140

Coca-Cola® Pecan Pie 116

Coca-Cola® Roast 54

Coca-Cola® Sloppy Joes 36

Coconut Shake 132

Country Captain Chicken 74

Creamy Caribbean Shrimp Salad 106

Creole Shrimp 72

Crostini with Eggplant Tapenade 10

Cuba Libre Chiffon Pie 118

Date-Nut Bread 124

Easy Coca-Cola® Chicken 62

Family Pot Roast 44

French Lentil Soup 25

French Onion Soup 22

Fresh Banana Cake with Seafoam Frosting 130

Fruited Pork Chops 56

Fudgey Coca-Cola® Brownies 120

Gazpacho with Coca-Cola® Reduction 12

German Sauerbraten 47

Ginger Chicken Wings 22

Gingerbread Deluxe.................... 138

Grecian Green Beans 102

Grilled Romaine Hearts with Tangy Vinaigrette 103

Hickory-Smoked Barbecue Chicken Wings......................... 26

Hoisin Chicken 78

Indian Chicken Curry 82

Italian Minestrone Soup 29

Italian-Style Vegetable Soup 18

Japanese Pickled Cauliflower 109

Limelight Steak BBQ 48

Marinated Pork Tenderloin 52

Matchless Meatloaf...................... 54

Mini Sliders with Coca-Cola® Caramelized Shallots 8

Mixed Fruit Compote 136

Mocha Coca-Cola® Float 118

Molten Lava Coca-Cola® Cakes 127

Mushroom Coca-Cola® Gravy....... 96

Mushroom-Barley Soup............... 19

Mustard Herb Dressing.............. 104

Pork Loin with Linguine................ 40

Roasted Potato Salad with Vegetables........................ 86

Scottish Oaten Bread 138

Seafood Gratin 78

Seafood Gumbo........................... 28

Seared Scallops with Coca-Cola® Glaze 80

Shrimp and Scallop Fettuccine 70

Sichuan Green Beans with Mushrooms 108

Smokehouse Barbecued Brisket 38

Southern Belle Salad 128

Southern Caramelized Vidalias 104

Spaghetti and Meatballs 30

Spice Island Chicken with Pineapple Rice 73

Spicy BBQ Party Franks 25

Spicy Pork Po' Boys..................... 42

Steak-Fried Onions...................... 92

Sweet and Sour Glazed Beef Kebobs.................................... 32

Sweet and Spicy Shrimp Tacos with Mango Salsa 64

Sweet Southern Barbecue Chicken 79

Sweet-Sour Cabbage................. 100

Teriyaki Chicken........................... 80

Thick Barbecue Sauce 92

Trio of Sweet and Spicy Dipping Sauces 88

Twin Cheese Dip.......................... 23

Uncle Joe's Baked Beans............. 98

METRIC CONVERSION CHART

VOLUME MEASUREMENTS (dry)

1/8 teaspoon = 0.5 mL
1/4 teaspoon = 1 mL
1/2 teaspoon = 2 mL
3/4 teaspoon = 4 mL
1 teaspoon = 5 mL
1 tablespoon = 15 mL
2 tablespoons = 30 mL
1/4 cup = 60 mL
1/3 cup = 75 mL
1/2 cup = 125 mL
2/3 cup = 150 mL
3/4 cup = 175 mL
1 cup = 250 mL
2 cups = 1 pint = 500 mL
3 cups = 750 mL
4 cups = 1 quart = 1 L

VOLUME MEASUREMENTS (fluid)

1 fluid ounce (2 tablespoons) = 30 mL
4 fluid ounces (1/2 cup) = 125 mL
8 fluid ounces (1 cup) = 250 mL
12 fluid ounces (1 1/2 cups) = 375 mL
16 fluid ounces (2 cups) = 500 mL

WEIGHTS (mass)

1/2 ounce = 15 g
1 ounce = 30 g
3 ounces = 90 g
4 ounces = 120 g
8 ounces = 225 g
10 ounces = 285 g
12 ounces = 360 g
16 ounces = 1 pound = 450 g

DIMENSIONS

1/16 inch = 2 mm
1/8 inch = 3 mm
1/4 inch = 6 mm
1/2 inch = 1.5 cm
3/4 inch = 2 cm
1 inch = 2.5 cm

OVEN TEMPERATURES

250°F = 120°C
275°F = 140°C
300°F = 150°C
325°F = 160°C
350°F = 180°C
375°F = 190°C
400°F = 200°C
425°F = 220°C
450°F = 230°C

BAKING PAN SIZES

Utensil	Size in Inches/Quarts	Metric Volume	Size in Centimeters
Baking or Cake Pan (square or rectangular)	8×8×2	2 L	20×20×5
	9×9×2	2.5 L	23×23×5
	12×8×2	3 L	30×20×5
	13×9×2	3.5 L	33×23×5
Loaf Pan	8×4×3	1.5 L	20×10×7
	9×5×3	2 L	23×13×7
Round Layer Cake Pan	8×1½	1.2 L	20×4
	9×1½	1.5 L	23×4
Pie Plate	8×1¼	750 mL	20×3
	9×1¼	1 L	23×3
Baking Dish or Casserole	1 quart	1 L	—
	1½ quarts	1.5 L	—
	2 quarts	2 L	—